Dad Desperately In Need Of Training Wheels

Paul A. Stankus

Copyright © 2012 Paul A. Stankus

All rights reserved. Copyright 2012 by Paul A. Stankus, Cover art by Blanca Cervantes. Inside photo credits: Paul A. Stankus, Candice Stankus, Alexander Stankus, and AnnMarie Wetherbee.

All rights reserved. Except as permitted under the U.S. Copyright Act of 1976, no part of this publication may be reproduced, distributed, or transmitted in any form or by any means, or stored in a database or retrieval system, without prior written permission of the author.

For previews of upcoming books from Paul A. Stankus, please visit his website at www.paulstankus.com.

ISBN: **1469943727**
ISBN-13: **978-1469943725**

Also available in Kindle, Nook, and iPad ebook versions

Dedication

To Candice and Alex,

From the moment you have walked into my life, you have changed it for good.

Preface

"Roll Over. Let me measure you."

I had been getting used to these rather insane-sounding requests from my seven-months pregnant wife. We were lying on the floor of our light green, freshly-painted nursery looking up at the ceiling when she got the brilliant idea that the crib was my length and twice my width and proceeded to drag me around the room as a crib proxy.

This is the husband's role during pregnancy. She is carrying your child; the least you can do is roll around on the floor for her.

I learned very early on – that as much as the partner wants to be there for the wife giving birth – that it's really her show-- and we're just along for the ride. So I attended to her in the best way I could.

I became a fact-o-matic pest – sorta like a guy who memorizes fantasy baseball stats for his favorite sports teams—only my stats were trimesters and weeks.

...Which probably wasn't what she had in mind when she asked me to come with her to the doctor's office for the checkups. Between each visit, I read a variety of those baby books that you usually see discretely tucked under a mother-to-be's arm—'What to Expect when You're Expecting,' 'Happiest Baby on the Block,' etc. I would start reeling off some of the useful nuggets I had learned about what was going on inside of her, to be met with a withering stare and a not so subtle non-verbal reminder that this was her body, not mine.

All mothers, including mothers-to-be, can disarm you with just a single laser piercing glance. It's an integral basic instinct honed from watching too many generations losing a hand in the fire. Husbands and sons, all of us, have never quite figured that out, and we blindly stumble into whatever danger presents us.

On one of these trips that the doctor said that at this stage of pregnancy, if you listen closely you can hear the heartbeat of your baby—so I leaned in for a closer listen. Instead of hearing the heartbeat, I saw stars as my future soccer fullback kicked me in the head.

This was the first of many, future interactions with our child. Before he was out of the womb, he was already walking all over me. I may be book-smart, but I still have a lot to learn about raising a child. I am the hapless papa-- the dad desperately in need of training wheels. Over the last six years I have written over 200 short stories chronicling Alex's life in flash-frame during my daily commute on the Metro train to downtown Washington, DC. These are my stories.

About This Book

Dad Desperately In Need of Training Wheels is written from the perspective of a first-time Dad interacting with his son, focusing on the camera-flash vignettes that punctuate our day-to-day existence.

This book is comprised of three parts: First Year (Getting to know Alex, and Candice and my reactions to being first-time parents.), Subjects (I grouped events as chronological within each category—food, sleep, diapers, work, life and daycare, etc.), and Reflections (My thoughts and observations of the special moments I want to remember.) It is an expansion of my earlier book, Hapless Papa.

I finished writing Dad Desperately In Need of Training Wheels the morning of Alex's sixth birthday. Happy Birthday, son.

Contents

	Acknowledgments	1
1	The Diaper Goes Where?	3
2	Herky-Jerky Motions of a New Dad	15
3	Wobbling Through Life	23
4	Three Ring Circus with Hungry Animals	34
5	Master of the Diaper Disaster	48
6	Sleep…Sleep…Please Sleeeeeeeeep	63
7	Don't Leave Dad Alone with Kid	77
8	Collisions Between Work and Life	94
9	Day Care Misadventures	103
10	Fun in the Sun or a Pain in the Breech	119
11	Baby Banter	137
12	Not All Fun and Games	159
13	A Sprinkle of Extraordinary	168
14	Learning Moments	199
15	Outsmarted!	210
16	Life Lessons	227
17	Father/ Son Moments	236
18	Five Minutes	252

Acknowledgements

While the stories of Dad Desperately In Need of Training Wheels are mine, the book would not have been possible without the help of the following people.

To Melissa, my writing editor, who challenged me to rethink many of my own premises about the book.

To my reviewers Dee, Tony, Anne Marie, and Ross, whose insightful comments found their way onto the pages.

To Mom, who labored over this book nearly as much as she edited the first, who made sure that my tone and context were correct.

To Julie, Tara, and Colleen, whose comments about which stories they liked and why kept me writing more.

To the patrons of the Washington DC Metro Redline daily for the last 6 years while I wrote in silence in the last car of the train.

Finally, this book would not have been possible were it not for my wife, Candice, and our son Alex, who provided all of the creative input for the snapshots in time that became the foundation stories in this and the previous book Hapless Papa. Thank you for being in my life every day.

Paul A. Stankus

1. The Diaper Goes Where?

Fathers -to- be think we know what we are doing. We don't. We may have been present at conception, and offer a supporting role during the pregnancy—but until that first diaper is fired, you really don't have any idea what parenthood is really like. Unlike mothers who talk endlessly with daughters about raising a child, most fathers are especially non-communicative about the process—as if it is as much a mystery to them as it is to you. Somewhere along the line we expect the next generation to forge ahead in through the nursery in the wilderness and build a new strong child at the end like a log cabin using only a couple of twigs.

If fathers were completely left in charge, the human race would have died out generations ago. Luckily, mothers save us from ourselves.

To a guy, duct tape solves most any problem. It is always better to let it out than to keep it in, and inanimate objects are carried best when they are carried like a football-- pretty much the exact opposite advice you want to use when dealing with a newborn. We have no idea what each whimper means. We freeze when a baby cries—(Is it gas? Is it hunger? Is it a shadow on the wall? Is it a diaper emergency? What? What?) All we can usually mutter is "baby's crying" as we search for the international baby translator – mom—who has gone off for some quiet and solitude in the form of a bubble bath. She trudges back, scowling, "Diaper. All yours," and returns to the inner sanctum, closing the door brusquely.

Ask almost any mother—she can 'name that cry' in three notes.

I have always been a bit of a nervous nelly when it comes to things outside of my control. I worry and fret and pace, as if by those actions I could control the world around me. My wife Candice's pregnancy was no exception. Having been a month-early baby myself, after the 8th month of watching the belly grow, every groan or utterance emanating from her sent me off to warm up the car and grab the birthing bag containing various "necessary" items for our half hour journey to the hospital.

(I've since found out after Alex was born that we used exactly three items from that bag—and that the real reason for all of the breathing exercises the birthing classes teach you have absolutely nothing to do with the mother—it is all to give the FATHER something to do so the mother does not strangle him by asking inane questions like, "Does it hurt?" And while I disagree with passing out the cigars, there are reasons previous generations of fathers stayed safely out in the waiting room.)

It sounds cliché, but the night of Alex's arrival was a nearly single- digit brain-freeze cold spell in the middle of February. We already had one false alarm this week, and a follow-up visit earlier today, but even the car was protesting as we made the silent journey at 1AM to the hospital. These sleepless nights were training for what we were about to experience over the next several months.

Candice patted her tummy. "Just think, this time tomorrow, we may have little Alexandra in our arms."

"Alexander," I corrected her.

It was a game we had played multiple times over the previous three months, ever since the two different sonogram technicians said, "I think it's as girl," and the doctor said, "Heartbeat's high—I think it's a boy." Candice clued in on "girl" and I clued in on "I think" – so of course she told everyone, "We're having a girl, but Paul is still holding out for a boy." A long time ago, we had picked the name Alex, which can work for either a boy or a girl name--just in case.

In preparing for the baby's arrival, Candice had gotten a little bit pink-crazy: Pink hats, pink onesies, pink booties, pink blankets, pink curtains, pink everything. Pink. Pink. Pink. Pink. Everything had to be pink. No daughter of hers was going to come home in anything less than full pink regalia. Even her mother, a former little girl's fashion designer, got into the act, resurrecting her clothing line and sewing several items of pink kiddie couture for Alex to come home in. We were the only patients in the wing that night, and we amused the nurses with a baby clothes fashion show, complete with 'OOOs' and 'AHHHs' as each item was shown. It was a veritable maternity ward fiesta.

The big moment arrived. Out popped Alex. As the doctors attended to him, I caught a glimpse of the tiny wiggling baby.

"Was it???" I wondered. "Could it really be?"

I angled for a better view.

It was. Exactly as I had hoped and wished for all these many months. Suddenly I blurted out,

"IT'S A BOY! IT'S A BOY!"

The nurses all stopped what they were doing, wheeled around and in unison exclaimed: "It's a WHAT?!?!?!?!?"

My mother was in the waiting room as she heard me shout. I met her at the door with tears streaming down my cheeks. "I'm in so much trouble," I said to her. Who knew, at the time, how prescient those words would be.

The doctor handed him to me. I held my newborn son in my arms and cried. Candice and I looked at him and said, "Isn't he the cutest baby ever born?" I knew right then that as much as she wanted a girl, that she would love her little boy with all of her strength.

Of course, had she not returned all of the gender-neutral clothing that friends gave her and bought pink, the gods would probably have granted her request for a girl. We call that hubris.

The day after my son was born, Candice remained in the hospital learning to care for a newborn. I, however, having not slept in 36 hours had the more challenging task: gathering up the mountain of pink at the house and returning it to the various stores for something better befitting a boy. (Mercifully, the color of the nursery was the *only* battle I won during the pregnancy—pale green is easily converted to either girl OR boy décor; otherwise I would have been repainting too in the midst of all this chaos. I can only imagine what kind of fanciful designs would have appeared unintentionally on the walls if I had mixed no sleep and paint fumes.)

I readily admit that I have absolutely no fashion sense whatsoever, so I enlisted the help of my mother for the daunting task at hand. At each store we visited, the conversation went something like this:

> *(Deep Breath) "Up until yesterday we thought we were having a girl. Yesterday we had a boy. Need to exchange all of this for the same items in blue. Is any of this yours and will you pleeeeeeeeeeeeeeease take it back?" (Exhale)*

I can only imagine what the salespeople thought – seeing this wild-eyed, bedraggled man with a Miami-Vice stubble beard and making as much sense as a babbling baboon screeching and gesturing in their store. Thankful that no one called the guys in the white coats for me that day, I visited several stores up and down Rockville Pike. Every couple hours we returned to the hospital to see how Candice was doing, and show her what we had purchased – to be greeted with a "You bought what????" and a stare that could melt military-grade steel. Back to the stores we'd go to return what we just bought. By the end of the day, the salespeople in one Pottery Barn Kids store greeted us with "Hi Alex's Grandmother" and "Hi Alex's Dad," their half-smiles confirming for me that we had definitely become the topic of the day in the break room.

I think it was in those frantic moments that I realized that I was no longer just Paul; I had been bestowed with a new title: "Alex's Dad." My world – and my place in the world-- had changed completely in the blink of an eye. I had become a father.

After two days in the hospital giving us as many lessons on parenting and baby care as we could cram in, the hospital staff wished us well and tossed us out into the really cold – 22 degree – world. Our breath frosted over as we took the few steps from the warm hospital to the car while Alex wailed in protest. Today was the day we would bring Alexander Paul home. It was a day we had been looking forward to for many months.

All traces of pink had been excised from the house, compliments of my mother. Fresh blue and green curtains were hung, bedding changed out—nothing at all to remind us that less than two days earlier the baby's room was pink enough for the prettiest princess in the kingdom. Too soon, though, the well-wishers departed and as the sun set and it was just the three of us. Candice went to get some rest and I was on duty.

I sat in the room on that bitter-cold winter night and could not get Alex to sleep. I rocked and I sang, and swooshed and everything—and still could not get him calmed down. Every time I laid him in the bassinette, he would wail, and flail and scream himself hoarse. I'd pick him back up and he would calm down a bit—but every time I'd lay him down he'd start wailing all over again. I went through the checklist, diapers--OK--milk--OK--holding him in my arms--OK--everything I had read I should do—but nothing was working. Candice, herself not having slept more than a few winks in the last 48 hours, awoke and stumbled down the hall muttering something.

By 4AM, neither Candice nor I could calm him down. I broke into my "in case of emergency package," pulled out the pacifiers that I had vowed to never use and started boiling them. It didn't work. He spit it out and continued to cry. I started to cry too—not because he was crying but because of my own failures in fatherhood. I thought I was ready to ride the bike of parenthood at full speed. Turns out I still needed training wheels and there were none to be found. I was the hapless papa—the completely incompetent fool not knowing which end of the diaper was up that I'd laughed at so many times before and vowed never to become.

Less than an hour later, exhausted and beyond tears, I finally found the only thing that could calm him down—the exhaust fan in the bathroom. (The exhaust fan? Really? Yes, really. I was surprised as much as you are.) I turned out the lights, turned on the fan, and rocked Alex to sleep.

Looking out the bathroom door, I could see the first rays of sunlight climbing over the tops of the townhouse roofs beyond and illuminating the silhouette of my sleeping infant. I felt a tear roll down my cheek as I cradled my newborn son in my arms -- we had all survived till morning.

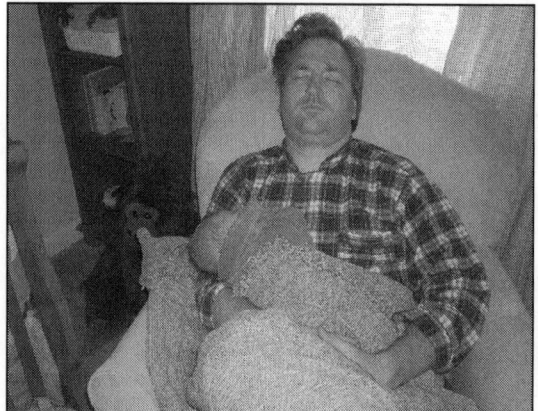

After a long night of crying, Dad is passed out in chair with Alex.

The first few weeks of a baby's life can be traumatic—if not just for the baby, freshly ripped from the mother's womb, but for the parents as well. Want to know why everyone always coos over sleeping babies? It's the only time that you get any down time – and even then, every new parent carefully peers over the edge of the bassinette making sure the child is still breathing. It's a delicate dance—checking on the child, without waking the child. Some parents I know have resorted to holding mirrors to the baby's nose – (They have a breath so they are good to go, right?)—so they can get positive verification without actually touching the infant— because once they're up, they're up—and so are you.

After about two weeks of sleep deprivation, parents start resorting to all kinds of trickery to gain a few more moments of shut eye. There's the negotiation: "I'll take the day shift, you take the night shift," the abdication: "If I lay here quietly long enough, he'll get up and take care of the baby," the elbow bump/ knee bump: "Well, since you're awake can you take care of the kid?" and my favorite, the Old West quick draw: "Baby's crying—your turn to get him," whereby the first one who says it, wins, and gets to go back to sleep. Inevitably, Candice had the quicker reflexes overnight and I'd get up and trudge down the hall.

One early morning before sunrise at 5:30 AM, I woke up to change Alex, giving Candice a few minutes more rest before she could feed him. In the brief seconds between me taking off the messy diaper and placing the clean one on him, he managed to kick off the covering, and spray the wall, the curtains, the changing pad and himself with yellow liquid. I started over-- with a now-screaming infant who had just peed all over himself and startled himself awake. Of course, with the changing pad soaked, I had to find an alternate location to change him – so off to our bedroom I went--naked, flailing child in hand.

And then he did it all again.

In the brief seconds between me laying him down on the bed, he managed to pee out of the diaper -- all over the bed, all over the clothes, all over himself—escalating the volume of crying in the process. By this time Candice is now wide awake, the child is screaming, the bed, the curtains, the wall, the changing pad, two outfits, three diapers, and the child all have pee on them. We start over for a third time-- this time Candice was changing him and I was changing everything else. The sun rose with me doing laundry trying to prevent the odor of "l'eau d'infant" from permeating the room.

A wise person once told me, when you are riding downhill it is often easy to lose control. In more than one way that person was correct-- it may get easier each day to care for a child, but on the way down, we have so many opportunities to go off course. It is always best to clamp on the training wheels, sit back and enjoy the passing scenery as it whizzes by.

~@~

My son gets plenty of "tummy time" - what doctors recommend babies do to strengthen their muscles and skeletons a couple of times a day. In Alex's case, he gets it considerably more, because at a month, he still refuses to sleep on his back and will only sleep on his stomach—which we discovered after a long night of crying when my mother flipped him over on his front and he fell instantly asleep. I've resigned myself to the fact that my son has his own way of doing things and that, contrary to the wishes of the self-help books, the doctors, and the other health workers, Alex will do what is most comfortable to him. I'm just so ecstatic that he's sleeping mostly through the night (though, slightly paranoid father that I am, still secretly checked on him in the middle of the night to make sure he hasn't smothered himself in his blanket). Five, six, or seven hours of sleep in a row—I feel like the King of Egypt.

We started to see a change in Alex's behavior by the fourth week. Every night around 3AM, we've started hearing a THUMP and a startled cry which sends us flying out of bed to investigate. Alex had figured out how to roll himself over—but hasn't figured out how to roll back leaving him "turtled". The first three nights of this, we congratulated him gave him a hug and put him back to bed. Tonight the clock struck three and right on cue, he flipped.

As suspected, he had rolled over, so I picked him up and gave him a hug, put him back down in the crib and slowly shuffled back to bed. I had no sooner fallen asleep, when I again heard: Thud! Rattle!

"WaaAAAahh."

Throwing over the covers, I got up and checked on him. Again, he had rolled over. Again, I picked him up and put him back down. Again, I trudged back to bed. And sure enough, just as my eyes were closing ten minutes later, he did it once more.

I lay in bed pulling the covers over my head, muttering something barely comprehensible, refusing to leave the warm blankets. As I remained ensconced in the covers, I hear on the monitor:

> *"Waaaaa?*
> *Waaaaah?*
> *Waaaaaaaahh?"*

I know those voice inflections by now. That wasn't a demand—it was a QUESTION.

Baby-speak Translation: I'm waiting for my applause line. Will you come pick me up?

It took every ounce of willpower in my body to not leave him "Turtled."

Now, I'm all for learning new skills, but isn't there some rule that new skills can only be learned between the hours of 7 AM and 9 PM?

2. Herky-Jerky Motions of a New Dad

Spring arrived with Alex's second month. The days were getting longer, the thermometer was getting longer, and most important of all, the sleeping through the night was getting longer still. I had been pulling double duty since Alex's birth--coming home from a long day at the office where I handle complaints for a large quasi non-profit, change clothes, and immediately assume my role as primary care giver to give Candice a much-needed break. She had the day shift. I have the night shift. On more than one occasion, I had stumbled out the door in the morning wearing my shirt inside out and thought it looked fine in the mirror when I got dressed.

For those of you without children, your mind starts playing tricks on you when you have gone for several days without sleep. Imagine what happens after several weeks of the same pattern? At one point I thought I looked like William Hurt in the mirror, but was quickly disabused of that notion. You learn very quickly that spell check is your friend, and that if people are asking you to repeat things, it's only because what seems to be making sense to you, is coming out as completely garbled and rambling to the outside world.

In this environment, I found myself one evening sitting at the dinner table trying to eat a bowl of spaghetti with one hand, and with the other, attempt to keep the rocking swing still rocking, while keeping the pacifier in his mouth. (One day soon he will hopefully learn cause and effect -- but for now it is just a surprise when the pacifier pops out.) Problem is the batteries were just starting to die on the portable swing, having been used so much over the last month. Every time I set the auto-rocker rocking, and attempt to wolf down a couple of bites, either the rocker would stop rocking, or the pacifier would fall out, resulting in a very LOUD demanding wail that needed immediate attention to.

Now, I have never been accused of being light on my feet-- I can walk down the sidewalk and fall off the edge—so it should come as no surprise that juggling complex feats of eating and timing the reinsertion of a pacifier into the mouth of a screaming infant swinging back and forth in a chair sends me into a spastic, uncoordinated fit. I straddled the chair, trying to feed myself with one hand and time the asymmetrical herky-jerky swinging motion with the other. Every time I tried to guide the pacifier, I would miss his open mouth or smush it into his closed mouth causing him to cry more. Finally, with one last effort and the grace of a greased bulldozer, I lunged for his open mouth wailing at full throttle, and in mid-thrust, realized that I had pushed too far. The supports of the chair skid out from under me and instead of successfully inserting the pacifier, found the hard tiles rapidly advancing on my face--much to the bemusement of Candice who had been watching the whole scene bug-eyed and giggly from the chair next to me the entire time.

Standing over me, she took the pacifier out of my hands, stopped the swing, and with a simple thrust, scored a direct hit in the mouth of the child, and clipped the end to his froggy outfit. She looked at Alex, glanced back at me lying prostrate on the floor, sending her into another fit of suppressed laughter, and promptly skittered off out of the room. I could hear her snort-laugh so hard she was gasping for breath as she hid behind the wall to the dining room. No sooner had she disappeared that Alex yanked his pacifier out again, startling himself into a wail. I crawled towards him, grimacing from my own bruised and battered body, and the piercing sound coming from the infant that can best be described as a six-alarm fire bell, ready to stop the swing one more time. He looked up and focused on me, this fuzzy dark shape advancing on him, located the pacifier, and stuck it back in his mouth. The look on his face spoke volumes: 'Thanks, Dad, but if you don't mind, I've got this one.'

A couple weeks later we saw my mother for Easter, and mom presented me a package she had been saving for a while that included my Christening dress (that she hoped would get used once again), my baby album, several handmade, crocheted outfits from when I was crawling around, and a photo taken by my grandfather when I was very little in the same outfit.

For Mother's Day, we returned the favor to Mom, taking several pictures of Alex in the 1970s style handmade teddy-bear style shorts and suspenders (after we got it properly dry cleaned, of course—I don't know where mom kept the outfit all of these years. Some things are better left unsaid). Using a bunny rabbit as a book end, we propped Alex up on the couch so we could snap some quick shots.

Candice glanced over my shoulder as I snapped the photos and noticed the photo taken by my Grandfather on the table we had been using as a template to stage Alex. She remarked at the fairly obvious similarities, "I want a maternity test. I'm sure he's yours, but I'm not sure he's mine."

At that moment, I wheeled around, and said to her in my best Austin Powers/ Dr. Evil voice, "I shall call him Mini-Me," and put my pinkie to the corner of my mouth as I scooped him up. Alex in turn, placed his own pinkie to his mouth, proving that he, indeed, was my clone.

~@~

It took several weeks, but I was finally beginning to adapt to my new fatherhood routine. Alex mostly slept through the night and I was only getting up three times an evening to feed and change him. I could sleepwalk to the kitchen, heat up one of the frozen milk bags that now overflowed in our freezer, feed, and change him all without waking up. I could even tell when his nighttime cries were real, or if they were just baby stirrings and startlings. Half the time I passed out in the rocking chair waiting for him to fall back asleep before I even made it back to bed. But, I've been told, progress is progress.

Even progress gets old after a while. You yearn for more advancement, for them to do things themselves—a tad unrealistic for an eight week old, I'll admit—but we can still have wishful thinking. I had listened to *thump*turtle*waaaaaa* for the better parts of three weeks and determined that I was going to do something about it. So on the second turtling of the night, I reached in and helped him roll over. Then I put him back where he was and repeated the process multiple times to give him some muscle memory.

The next day I watched him in the crib as he rolled over, tucking his arm in like I showed him and getting through a whole revolution—one complete flip from front to back to front again. Within a couple of days it had changed from *thump*turtle*waaaaaa to thump (pause) roll, thump (pause) roll from one end of the crib to the other. I was deliriously happy in his new found skills until he located the musical baby aquarium at the end, and bumped up against it, setting off "Twinkle, Twinkle Little Star."

Later that week when he completely comprehended that he could turn on the music with a swat of his hand, and play it over, and over, and over again, I covered my head with the pillow to drown out its 832nd performance still ringing in my ears.

So what was I saying? Oh that's right—"Progress is progress." Be careful what you wish for.

~@~

"Mrs. Stankus... this is (the daycare provider) calling. We have Alex scheduled to start with us on September 1. Please let us know if you wish us to hold Alex's spot. ..." The message continued, but all I heard was September 1. The deposit we had given the daycare provider was for JUNE 1, not September 1. I replayed the message multiple times. Had I heard it wrong? The sweat beaded up on my forehead. We were just four weeks shy of Candice returning to work from maternity leave, and now, we have no daycare provider.

In the Washington DC area, daycare centers are very competitive. Spots fill up quickly for some of the more prestigious schools, the good at-home daycares have long waiting lists, and those without waiting lists might be operating in a less than official capacity. When we were interviewing with some of the schools we were told that there was a substantial deposit fee, and that there was a waiting list of over a year to get in?

Over a year? How is that even possible?

Assuming that the baby takes nine months to pop out like most babies do, and that maternity leave generally lasts about three months, a waiting list of over a year means that for some of the higher-end schools, your spot on the list must be secured before the child is CONCEIVED.

...And so we scrambled. We began frantically calling every single provider on the list controlled by the county. I felt like such the bad parent. Even though I had made arrangements nearly eight months prior, the questions I was asked made it seem that I had waited until the very last moment to arrange for child care, that I was careless and irresponsible - completely the opposite of the exhaustive and methodological process I had gone through the first time we chose Alex's caretakers. I was being interviewed as much if not more than I was interviewing them. They wanted to know who we were, where we lived, how we parented, etc. Finally, after two frantic weeks of searching, we found someone in our neighborhood who would take him in. Walking distance! Our problems were solved!

Or so I thought. The gods have a fickle sense of humor. There was one small--and by small, I mean pretty gargantuan new issue to overcome with the new daycare—the fact that the new daycare's day ends precisely at 6PM. If you are not there when the clock strikes 6 or sooner, you owe additional "incentive fees"—the incentive being a dollar a minute you are late, on top of your monthly fees (to "incentivize" you to be there on time, of course). I've since learned this is standard practice in our area—with some facilities charging up to $5 a minute late fee so that all of the type A personalities who live and work in DC don't make the calculation that if their billables are $200 an hour, that they can afford to be an hour late to pick their child up from day care. After all, nannies and child care workers have lives of their own. As I had been planning on a much later pick up time, I scrambled to change my work schedule around so I could be there before closing. Over the next two weeks while I adapted to the hour earlier schedule, (and consequently an hour less sleep than I was already getting) I showed up to the office on two separate days with mismatched socks, one shirt on inside out, and one shirt with buttons askew. But in those few weeks I learned that happiness comes from unexpected times and places. I found that once I adapted to the changes going on around me, that I enjoyed the one-on-one alone time I had with Alex in the baby carriage on the 15 minute walk home. To pass the time, I came up with a rather loopy, sing-songy song that I repeated over and over again that went something like this:

Alexander, he's so great. No one else, can relate. Alexander, he's so great. He's the one the girls want to date. Alexander he's so great. I'm on the train so I won't be late. So I can play with Alexander, the Great.

The only person who seemed to mind was the grandmother watering her flowers as we passed by, who grimaced and groaned as she heard the song each day. What did I care though? It may have been loopy and borderline criteria for a psychiatric evaluation, but at least it made Alex smile.

~@~

3. Wobbling Through Life

During the first year of a child's life there's a lot of crying going on, and not all of it coming from the crib. He's tired, Candice is tired, I'm tired--and when everyone is tired, we are all Neanderthal-like and non-communicative.

It took me a bit of time, but I can finally begin to differentiate between the **"Feed me NOW"** cry, the **"diaper's flooded"** cry, the **"scary shadow on the wall"** cry, and the **"I'm-so-tired-that-I-don't-want-to-go-to-bed-even-though-mom-and-dad-are-nearly-passed out"** cry.

Mom, of course, had plenty of experience attuning to the cries, but I was at work most of the day and did not have as much practice getting down the nuances of the pitch, tone, and context as she did. To be sure, I did my share of exhausted, fatigued, frustrated crying out that first year. For every cry I uttered in pain or despair, I uttered two in wonder and surprise, so by that crude calculation, I think I came out ahead.

Around five months, lots of things began to change—both of Alex, who was no longer a lump of clay with a head and four wiggly appendages, but also of our relationship as he began to recognize who I was, who would turn towards me when I would call his name, who acknowledged the sound of my voice, reaching towards me as I approached the crib.

Of course, I didn't know it at the time, but it was a trap—for as soon as I reached in, he put his hand inside my pajamas shirt and ripped out a clump of chest hair. I can honestly tell you that there are times other than the birth of your son that a grown man will cry—and having your chest hair follicles forcibly and unexpectedly removed by an infant with a compression-clamp grip is guaranteed to bring a tear to any man's eye. I now have a better appreciation for this beauty procedure women subject themselves to called a bikini wax.

~@~

Another thing that changed at five months was Alex's eating habits. Up until then, Alex was fine with the bottle or mom, but once the emergence of the teeth occurred, all bets were off. Parenthood is all about pivoting quickly to events around you and adapting to an ever-changing environment—which in itself is ironic, since I spent so much time planning for the event, I never expected the urgent immediacy of caring for a child. The movies only show the frantic father rushing into the

Dad Desperately In Need of Training Wheels

delivery room at the last minute to be with mom as the baby arrives. They never show the father six months later trying to introduce the food to the pint-sized emperor, with a spoon for a scepter and an upside down bowl for a crown. We bow before the tiny tyrant, offering him carrots when he really wants applesauce—the thicker, slimier, and more viscous through his stubby fingers, the better-- and in his disdain, sends the carrots flying in a bright orange blast pattern of goo all over the floor.

After the first couple of misadventures, I learned quickly to invest in plastic tablecloths to place one under the high chair where the budding pitcher can wind up at his leisure and you don't have to worry about the mess. The next day, when the child decides he no longer likes the food you made for him

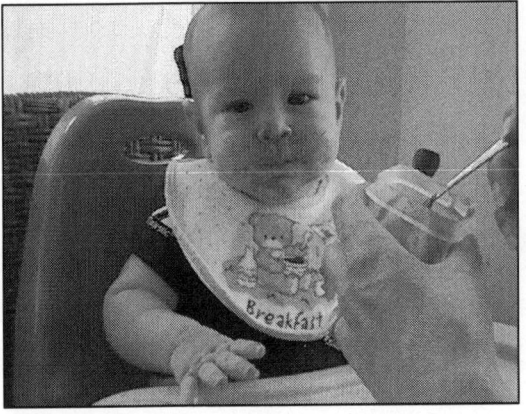

Orange Goo --it's not just for breakfast (or lunch, or dinner) anymore.

yesterday, and mom is nowhere in sight, you resort to making three different items, and whatever is not smacked away, is what they want that day. But when that third item goes flying, and the child is crying at the top of their lungs, you throw your hands up in despair and would gladly pay $1 million dollars for an accurate baby translator that could tell you what your baby wants.

One day while enduring the daily splatter, I think I finally figured out what he wanted. It wasn't necessarily the food he didn't like—it was the fact that I was feeding him. Every time he batted the spoon away, he puffed out his face like a bowling ball, making an expression I can best describe as, "ME DO IT." It wasn't that he didn't like the food. It was that he wanted to be the one to use the spoon to feed himself—for when the spoon was placed in his hands, it didn't matter what the food was (even if he had rejected it 10 minutes prior) it just mattered that he was in control of his own culinary destiny.

Our child isn't fussy about the food in front of him... he's being stubborn and independent. Once he sets his mind on something, he's not going to change his mind. ... And if you tried to change it for him...well that's what his vocal cords are for. Who needs talking? They say that 65% of the message is what's not said anyway—so you don't necessarily need to be a mind reader to be a baby whisperer— just get really good about interpreting their expressions.

Like the stable hand cleaning out the stalls, after-meal clean up consists of taking the blast mat outside and hosing it down. I bring the mat back inside, only to find that like paint droplets, the goo has slimed its way down into the carpet, creating multi-colored polka-dots on the rug. It's a good thing we keep the steam vacuum around.

We thought getting enough food inside of Alex instead of wearing it was our biggest challenge—which it was until he started to move—and move quickly. It started with a rolling motion when he would rotate over and over from one side of the rug to the other, and morphed into a soldier crawl on the floor, where Alex would reach forward, grab at the carpet and leg flop trying to flop himself forward a couple of inches like a fish out of water. To help him along, we assembled this bungee cord contraption mounted on four stilts and as big as an upholstered chair. It made "boing-boing" noises like a pogo stick and lit up whenever he bounced, which was apparently all he needed. No sooner did Alex's feet touch the ground that he discovered that he had feet and that feet could be useful for jumping up and down. Pretty soon he was squealing in delight and crying in surprise that he could actually make the bungee cord swing move around by simply pushing off on the ground. At one point, he was giggling and bouncing around so much I considered weighing down the legs of the Jumparoo, lest he turn it into a trampoline and go bouncing down the hall.

I extracted him from the exercise toy and wondered what would happen if I stood him up. He already had been using his compression clamp fingers on me, and had been pulling himself up using his baby jungle gym, so I took him over to the carpet, had him hold onto each finger and raised him to a standing position. Alex looked down and cried in surprise and delight. He had never seen the world before from this height, and more importantly, he had never seen his feet from that angle. I called out to Candice, "Come quick!" adding, "And bring the video camera."

I inched forward and he swayed and wobbled like a top about to tip over. It will still be a few more months before he can properly move his feet, so I lifted him up gently onto my toes and gently inched forward like a marionette. I moved ahead, he moved ahead. I moved to the right, he moved to the right in perfect unison. Each time we moved, he squealed in surprised approval at the adjustment in visual perspective.

By the time Candice arrived with the camera, we had gotten the routine down, and were able to walk across the room with no effort. Alex surprised even me, when by the end he attempted to take a step on his own, without the aid of his marionetted feet.

Simple Words

Rightfully or not, I consider a baby's first forming of words to be the most important milestones, because at that moment, he/ she begins to communicate to you what their needs are. Before that, you pretty much have to guess. It may be an educated guess, or a process of elimination guess, but it is still a guess nonetheless. Like most milestone moments, it sneaks up on you silently, catching you at your most unaware and willing to receive it.

The sun streamed a diffuse glow through the flimsy window coverings as I lay on the unmade bed one lazy Sunday morning in October. Candice had dropped Alex off on the bed for me to watch (and fully wake me up) while she started the laundry. He scooted around - ducking under pillows and burrowing into the bedcovers. I covered him up—and he would move around and find his way out, squealing and giggling each time.

I rolled over, grabbed my eyeglasses off the nightstand next to me, and propped up on my elbow to watch him as he struggled out from his man-made cave. He emerged, throwing the covers off with a disdainful heave and slinked his way over to me, grabbing my nose and a clump of hair to pull himself up to a standing position.

Alex looked me in the eyes, smiled, swatted me at the head and then said two simple words that took my breath away.

"Hi Daddy!"

A warmth of pride overwhelmed me as I lay speechless on the bed. Alex smacked at my eyeglasses and said it again. As quick as he had said it, he flopped down to the comforter and wandered to the other side of the bed. I watched as he resumed playing with the pillows and blankets.

And then it hit me. My eyes welled up. In an instant, those two little words made up for what seemed to be a lifetime of late-night feedings, sleepless nights and eternal vigilance.

My face went flush. It was at that moment that my own immense pride over really hearing his voice for the first time merged with my own slowly emerging realization that:
His first words were a complete sentence.

Photo taken moments after Alex said his first words.

~@~

Exploring within limits is an important part of growing up. When Candice worked her weekend job at the Kellogg Collection, a high-end furniture store in DC, she learned the concept of "the one-finger rule"— whereby an inquisitive child was permitted to touch an object with one finger, thus satisfying the child's need to touch, but also the store's need to not have expensive lamps broken. We adopted the same philosophy with Alex at home—setting aside things that he could touch, away from things that could hurt him. One thing we did was give Alex his own cabinet, full of bowls, bibs, bottles, pots and pans that he could play without getting conked on the head. Daily, he would crawl to the cabinet and pull everything out onto the tile floor, making a royal racket in the process. We didn't mind the clatter—it gave us an audio locator of where he was in the kitchen when he was out of eyesight.

Our ears perk up when the clatter stops. Any parent will tell you, that you don't listen for the noises-- you listen for the silence-- because that is the time that the kids are getting themselves in trouble by doing something that they shouldn't be doing. So when the clattering of the cups and bowls stopped, I immediately began searching, calling out through the kitchen, "Alex. Alex. ALEX" --each call, getting more insistent and more urgent. I rounded the island and looked down and saw two piggies dangling from inside the cabinet. I opened the cabinet door to find him, much to my relief, lying on his belly contentedly stacking bowls one-by-one on the shelves inside. He turned back, saw me and smiled, letting out a surprised cry and yelp, and went back to orderly stacking his bowls as if I never existed.

A few days later, Alex was playing his "baby grand" piano in the kitchen when you saw a glimmer of an idea of recognition spread across his face. He immediately crawled over to his cabinet, extricated a tin pot from its position on top of the pile, and dragged it back to the piano. He looked at it, decided it needed more "stuff" and crawled back to the cabinet to get a second pot. When that one was now in place, he sat in the middle – piano straight ahead, "drums" to the left and right-- and began to jam.

*bang*bop*bop*twinkle*twinkle*twinkle*

bang*bop*twinkle*bopbopbop.

He turned to me grinning happily as he just had performed the opening act of his one baby band.

Candice came down the stairs crying out, "What is all this racket down here?" To which I replied, "Music." We told my mother about his performance later that afternoon and she offered to get him a drum set, like the one my brother had growing up. I said "sure he can have a drum set—we'll keep it at your house and he can play it... when he comes to visit you."

Future musician? Only time will tell.

~@~

What started out as seemingly random cries, by the end of the year had turned into words. In looking back, their intentions were made clear not by the cries themselves, but by the meanings he attempted to communicate. I heard happy and scared cries, love and affection cries, snuggling cries, and cries just before he finally closed his eyes to sleep soundly on my shoulder. The whimpers and purses of his lips as he slept were the best cries of all.

This is one of my favorite photos, taken at Monticello with Candice, Alex, and me sitting on the roots of Thomas Jefferson's trees.

~@~

4. Three Ring Circus with Hungry Animals

Food. That which nourishes our bodies and makes us grow strong has many different uses for a child. It can be a toy, a projectile, an artistic implement, a measure of defiance, and a key of independence. Often the biggest battles we have with our children at a young age are those focused on food—whether it is getting them to try something other than the ubiquitous chicken nuggets and macaroni and cheese, or to eat because you know it's good for them, in spite of their protestations.

Since we are talking about food, I figured now would be a good time to explain to the readers that the first three chapters were more of a sampler platter of stories throughout the first year. The remaining chapters are grouped by subject (food, sleep, talking, etc.) because it is always better to keep the green beans separated from the mashed potatoes unless you are making Shepherd's Pie. And since I'm making myself hungry talking about sampler platters, I'm going to let you get back to reading. Pardon the interruption while I backtrack a bit.

Throughout the first few months of Alex's life, Candice had been his primary food supply. When I took over evening feedings, I alternated one milk bottle early in the night and one formula bottle later on. Our plan had always been to continue primarily breast feeding up until about nine months of age, which would give Alex a healthy start with the nutrients and anti-bodies essential in mother's milk.

Yeah... about that. We hadn't counted on the vampire fangs.

Alex was five months old, and he and I were on the couch playing with one of those too-numerous-to-count fuzzy animals that we've somehow acquired since he was born. Instead of grabbing the butterfly, he grabbed my fingers and shoved them into his mouth. Suddenly, I felt a searing pain.

Immediately I recoiled in shock. Two Grand-Canyon deep impressions, red and pulsing, had appeared on my finger. I looked in Alex's mouth. Sure enough, two sharp baby teeth had popped through. No longer sheathed in their mushy cocoon, they greeted my digits with a ritual bloodletting, causing me to recoil in pain, and him to recoil in surprise. The next day, Candice, unfortunately, also discovered the vampire fangs. With tears welling up in her eyes, and the unimaginable pain clouding her mind, she very quickly decided to abandon breastfeeding altogether-- lest she start to lose important body parts.

Suddenly, we were left without a plan B as his primary source or nourishment was now on the injured reserve list. We had planned to introduce solid foods slowly—but that plan was quickly accelerated. We raided the cabinet for the liquefied carrots. "Would he like it?" We wondered. Would he spit it out and demand the milk instead? Our doctors, family, friends and several baby books had said that it may take several weeks as the baby gets used to new foods and textures. In our case ... the transition took three (3)... spoonfuls.

The first spoonful he greeted with a quizzical look as if to say `what is this gruel,' the 2nd spoonful he sorta pushed around his mouth and the third he decided he liked it so much that he tried to jump out of his booster seat, lunging at the spoon and biting it with such vigor that I thought for certain he would have chomped the baby spoon in half were it not made of metal. Alex mercilessly attacked, demanding more and more sacrifices to his insatiable lust.

By the end of the carnage, he had grown a goatee of carrot purée to accompany his near-demonic possession. There were carrots in his hair, in our hair, on our clothes and laid out in a blast pattern around the booster seat. He opened his mouth so wide to receive this new food that I began to wonder if he had a flip-top head.

Broccoli Bombs Away

As a child, I remember my parents using different tactics on me—"train into the station" and "airplane coming in for a landing" making wide sweeping motions with their arms complete with sound effects. Candice remembers her own father trying with his bumbling attempts and getting her and her sister to eat with his "toys for the children" routine. Whatever the methods used, we parents spend an inordinate amount of time trying to encourage good food habits.

It's no wonder children expect to be entertained at dinnertime, and explains the success of restaurants like Chuck E. Cheese.

Alex was in his highchair eating lunch when he was about 18 months old. The day before, he had eaten every last bite of his broccoli and cheese—so not wanting to tempt fate, I again made him broccoli for dinner. But that was yesterday, not today—and the rules changed overnight. Try as I may, I have a hard time remembering what yesterday's rules were, much less today's—and you can just forget about me having any clue about tomorrow—which as a project manager who has to plan and anticipate actions several months out at my job, pretty much drives me insane at home.

I put the broccoli on his tray—luckily BEFORE I put the cheese sauce on it—and with a wide sweeping deliberate arc, he wipes it clean, winging the broccoli against the wall. I put it back on his tray, it goes flying again. I'm determined to get him to eat his vegetables – because now it's a matter of pride to bend him to my will.

"Eat it, it's good for you," I beg and plead.

At that moment, he looks me square in the eyes, waves his arms wildly like a home plate umpire: "All done. Get down now," and promptly smacks the broccoli hard enough to send pale green debris bomblets raining all over me and down onto the floor. I brush them off my glasses and my shirt where they have stuck to the lenses and the fabric like pricker bush seeds.

Alright. I get the point. You DON'T want the broccoli. You win.

~@~

Yucky

As my mother can attest from my early experiences in cooking at home, (just ask her about the time I turned two batches of zucchini bread into four cinder blocks and four million pieces that got me banished from the kitchen till well after I graduated high school) I could probably use some cooking lessons—and Alex, as helpful as he is, will remind me of it any chance he gets. Most times, if it doesn't come out of a bag, it doesn't get made. I keep the freezer fully stocked with stuff I can pull out and defrost. It's safer that way. No one gets food poisoning from food that has already been to Antarctica and back.

I should know better by now, but every once in a while I try something adventurous. Candice asked me to cook a pot roast in the crock pot. We filled it up in the morning and turned it on while we went to work. I didn't quite get around to putting optional things like seasonings, salt, pepper, or bouillon cubes—and the results showed. I scooped out Alex's plate and handed him his dinner. He took the fork in his hand, stabbed a piece of meat and took a bite. He scrunched up his face like a wrinkled old man who'd just smelled an over-ripe cabbage.

"Yucky..." he exclaimed.

"Oh come on, try it," I pleaded. "Have a bite of potatoes."

"Yucky....," he answered adamantly.

I took a bite for myself without really tasting it. "Ummm ...ummmm good. It's really good – I'm sure you want some," and handed him the fork.

Again he tasted it and spit it out.

Alex looks me in the eye, and says, "Tastes like Play-Doh."

I sat there with my mouth wide open and scraping my shoelaces for what was probably the better part of a minute, but felt positively glacial. I picked up the fork and tasted it again myself.

Sure enough, I've tasted better glue on a postage stamp.

~@~

Lini?

It was 5:30 PM and I had just picked up Alex from daycare. As I buckled him in the car, he asked me, "lini?" (tortellini) – which we had made for him the previous night.

"Yes, you can have more tortellini when we get home," I responded.

All the way home, he's singing, "Li-ne, LI-NE, LINI, LEENEE" and I assured him at least two dozen more times over the fifteen minute drive home that yes, he would get his tortellini.

We pulled in the driveway and I shut off the car. As soon as he cleared the car seat, he ran for the back door.

"Lini, Lini, Lini." He said as he pointed excitedly at the door, jerking his arm up and down with each inflection.

"YES, I'll make it right now," as I turned the keys in the lock.

Immediately, I started dinner, hampered only by the laws of physics and the inability to boil water faster. All the while, Alex is dancing and singing in the background about his Lini's. Breathless, and proud of myself for what is probably my world record in getting dinner ready – I presented him his plate.

Alex momentarily looks at the plate, and pushes it away—"NO!" he says loudly.

I push it back in front of him, "YES."

"NO!" He pushed it back and in the process turned the plate upside down, little tortellinis scattering all over the table.

I took a deep breath, clenched my fingers, and turned away, the smoke curling out of my ears. *'Must...Not...Throttle... Child.'* I repeated to myself while taking a second deep breath.

Alex watched me walk away. When I was halfway across the room, he reached over to the plate of overturned tortellini and popped one in his mouth, grinning wildly.

I momentarily left the room. If you listen carefully, you can probably still hear the echoes of my primordial screams drifting in the wind.

~@~

It's dinner time again. I can never guess right on the portion size for Alex. Either I guess high—and he eats two or three bites, or I guess low, and he demands more—and when I make him more it seems that his brain has caught up with the pixy size of his stomach and he only eats two or three bites of the 2nd helping. Either way, there's usually at least half a portion left.

Growing up, we didn't have that option—we ate what we took and were not excused until we finished it.

To this day, I still have trouble looking at a dinner plate and seeing food go to waste. So inevitably, I'll eat what's left on his plate as well. I've lost count of how many times I've ended up eating dinner on a plate with dinosaurs or little bunny rabbits. It's not that I have a chance to enjoy it- because no sooner do I start eating, Alex is off zipping around the house like a whirlwind. At least the indigestion is keeping me from eating everything in sight.

~@~

The Blue Raspberry Slurpee

Between two and three, many toddlers exert their independence. It's an age punctuated by sharp cries of, 'I WANT TO DO IT' - in spite of whether or not they are actually able to do so. At this age, they are more apt to attempt to pour the gallon of milk in a glass, but because they can't lift it, tip the milk jug over on the countertop, creating a gurgling, creamy waterfall puddle in the kitchen before you can dive underneath and save it.

Often I find myself in a precarious position—wanting to jump in and do something for Alex, but always cautiously optimistic that he will find a way to do it on his own. I'm learning to control my impulses to intervene, even if it means walking around for the next few hours with a blue raspberry slurpee -covered three-year-old who impetuously wanted to work the dispenser.

On one such night, the three of us had stopped by a local store to pick up some essentials, and treated ourselves to a shared slurpee. Alex was fascinated by

Dad Desperately In Need of Training Wheels

the slurpee-making contraption—he marveled at the levers, switches and scoops whirring in unison as the icy fruit concoction began to ooze out of the canister. Each time we went to sit down, he would wander back to the slurpee machine and watch the blades spin.

Suddenly he had an idea. A wonderful, mischievous idea I'm sure, because I could see the devil horns appear underneath his reddish blond cowlicks as he sauntered over to the condiments counter, reaching up to grab some napkins. I watched from a safe-ish distance (close enough to jump in to action in a split second, yet far enough away to let him accomplish his task), as he struggled with the box, nearly pulling it down on himself multiple times, but emerged victorious with several crunched in his hands.

"I'd like a smoothie for my mommy," he said to the cashier in pitch-perfect grammar, handing her the crumpled napkins substituting for dollar bills.

Quite taken with him, the cashier handed him a cup and watched him walk back to the slurpee machine. He reached up to turn on the slurpee maker—but could not reach the handles. Looking around, he spied the footstool, and dragging it over, clamored up the steps. Tugging and pulling, he managed to engage the clunky motor, and watched in fascination as the semi-frozen liquid began to dribble out.

I stood at a distance, watching the cup fill up with blue liquid. 'Would he turn it off on his own,' I wondered? Slowly the slushy levels grew higher and higher and I realized that he wasn't going to stop it, so I intervened. He looked at me defiantly and shouted, "No! I want to do it!" grabbing the cup away and splashing part of the contents out of the cup and all over the front of me. I stood there, grimacing as the multi-colored coldness seeped through my shirt as he delivered the slushie to Candice.

I questioned myself inside my head, 'Would he have stopped the slushie machine on his own if I had not intervened?' Had my attempts to prevent him from making a mistake, in fact caused the even bigger mess?

~@~

Communion Bread

As a young child, we attended church every Sunday. Occasionally, we would go up into the choir loft so the three of us children could see the ceremony. That lasted until, children being children; I bumped the hymnal off the ledge onto the head of the chief usher (who also happened to be our insurance agent) with a loud thud that drew the looks of nearly everyone in the congregation. Needless to say, that was the last time for me in the Choir loft. I see the apple doesn't fall far from the tree.

When Alex was fifteen months old, he developed a penchant for saying the word "cracker." Everything to him was a cracker—a piece of bread, a handful of goldfish, a pretzel rod—you name it, it was a cracker. If it could be grabbed and shoved in his mouth, it was hence now and forever more known as, a cracker. He toddled around saying "cracker, cracker, cracker" as he raided the cabinets in search of snacks.

At the end of the month, my grandfather passed away at the age of 90, and we traveled to Baltimore to attend his Catholic funeral Mass. We managed to keep Alex quiet and entertained in the pew until he looked up at the part of the service when the priest was blessing the Eucharist wafers. He immediately jumped up, excitedly pointed at the communion wafer, loudly saying "cracker, cracker, cracker," and bringing a smile to the congregation.

It was a fitting tribute to my grandfather-- who being slightly deaf could usually not tell how loud he was speaking as his voice echoed with his laughter with priests and fellow parishioners throughout the halls and corridors of the church he had served for over 50 years.

This is but one of Alex's run-ins with the Catholic Church. Another occurred several months later at St. Elizabeth's, a local church where Candice had been asked by friends of ours to stand up as a role model for their daughter at the First Communion ceremony (which is in itself, ironic, as Candice may be moral, but definitely not religious) to which she readily agreed—so long as she didn't have to become religious to participate.

The three of us arrived early that day so that Candice could fulfill her duties. She went off for pictures, and I remained at the playground watching Alex. The ground was muddy from the springtime rains the day before, and I spent the greater part of an hour diving unceremoniously to prevent a puddle jump or a mudslide that would have ruined his Sunday best outfit. In between exertions, I doled out the preplanned snacks that Candice had prepared the night before.

Mothers plan those types of things; Fathers just wing it. If it had been left up to me (which it wasn't) I probably would have ended up taking him down the street for pizza or something equally unhealthy. As it was, I had used up all the snacks a half hour before the event started, with a hungry child rooting around for more. I was expected to be in the pew. I couldn't just duck out now.

I had conveniently forgotten how long Catholic Mass is—particularly a special celebration like a First Communion, which contains all of the pomp and pageantry bringing a new member into the community. As most parents know, what may seem long for attendees is exponentially longer for toddlers, who have an attention span measured in seconds directly proportional to the number of months they are old. As the service droned on and on, the robed altar servers brought several gifts down the aisle and placed them on the small table in front. Included in these gifts were three large dinner rolls to be used for communion.

Before I could move a muscle, Alex had spied the dinner rolls and began climbing over the pew saying "ROLLS. I want rolls," and began running towards the table. I extricated myself from the pew and diving, intercepted him mid-reach within a foot or two of him taking a bite out of the First Communion bread. As I carried him out, his legs still pumping furiously, his body twisting and turning to escape, and him pointing to the table, he begins to wail, "BUT I WANTED THE BREAD."

And if you ever want to see how quickly an adult man can shuffle-run out the door, just watch the dagger eyes appear in the entire congregation as someone tries to make off with the communal meal they had gathered that day to celebrate.

~@~

5. Master of the Diaper Disaster

When Candice was about seven months pregnant, our family and friends threw her a surprise baby shower at our house. One of the games that the organizers had planned was "Diaper the Doll Race." Both Candice and I were given a doll, an old-fashioned cloth diaper, and a couple of safety pins. At the count of three, my sister started the stopwatch and we dropped down to all fours to change the doll. In record time, I whipped the old diaper off, folded it neatly away, cleaned up the doll, and put the new diaper on, beating Candice by a full 30 seconds. Triumphantly, I raised the baby doll up high and claimed victory—only to watch the diaper fall off the legs, leaving me to stare at a shiny plastic bottom. My smile turned to a frown. "Disqualified!" the guests shouted.

"Disqualified? How????" I asked.

"Diaper didn't stay on. You must start again,"

several participants interjected.

It was the closest I have ever come to winning at the diaper game—and it was definitely a warning premonition of what was to come.

I am what one would charitably call, the "Master of the Diaper Disaster." While Candice can change a hundred diapers without breaking a sweat, I change one and all kinds of literal and figurative stuff hits the fan. More often than not, the tiny wiggling baby turns into a greased pig the second the diaper comes off, and I end up trying to keep him still with one hand while changing him with the other hand.

For someone who can barely master the art of walking and talking at the same time, this new foray into feats of dexterity often ends up with either a partially diapered child with one leg swinging free, or a diaper destroyed by the tabs ripped off in frustration. During the first few months, it was not uncommon for me to use double or triple the number of diapers I was expecting to use. Every once in a while, Candice would peek in and ask not so innocently and partially accusatory, "Where did all the diapers go so quickly?" to which I would point meekly to the diaper pail in the corner and make plans for another Costco run. It seems that we visit there almost every other week. Between the diapers and the powdered formula for nighttime feedings, we single-handedly keep that big box store in business.

Diapers in bulk. You need them for a newborn—

sometimes a dozen a day. No wonder the most popular decoration at baby showers is the diaper pyramid. You may laugh, but when it's 3AM and you are changing your child for the tenth time since you woke up today, you'll be glad when you have a stockpile to draw from.

One can never have too many diapers on a road trip. For Mother's Day, we made the trek to my parents' house outside of Philadelphia, PA, a short three hours away. It had been an eventful trip as Alex caught a flu bug and was generally feeling crummy. Normally, he is a good sleeper in the car, having acquired his mother's penchant for falling asleep as soon as she is buckled in as a passenger in a moving vehicle. This time, however, he was wide awake moaning and groaning with tummy troubles—which is parental code for, "It's coming out one end or the other--you just don't know which end yet." We got about halfway home and Alex let out a wail. I adjusted the driver mirror and looked down at him in the back seat as I watched the sides of his outfit starting to turn a brownish mustard color. I turned to Candice, who was nestled in partial slumber-land beside me in the front seat.

'You awake over there? Alex needs some attention," I called out urgently.

I nudged Candice and she either ignored me or continued to pretend she was asleep. I nudged her again. Getting no response, I looked down, saw the edges spreading and did what any father traveling at highway speeds would do – threw the flashers on and tried to get to the side of the highway. With luck, no one was in my way, so I guided the car to a halt on the side of the road in the midst of traffic zipping by.

Candice woke up from both the sudden deceleration and the loud mournful wail coming out of the back seat. I hopped out of the car and ran around to the non-traffic side of the car to take care of Alex.

I no sooner opened the door, and the poor diaper could not hold any more and burst at the seams, muck puddling everywhere – in the car seat, all over his front, sides and back, and then, when he put his hands in it, in his hair as well.

I dove for the diaper bag and opened the wipes to find that there were two wipes left in the package—not nearly enough to clean him up. I yanked him out of the car seat and proceeded to wipe him off the best I could—which was absolutely no help whatsoever until I got the idea of pouring a bottle of water on him – so I held him out at a distance while Candice gave him a quick shower with the water bottle from the car.

Alex bellowed in protest. I stripped off his soaking wet clothes and dried him off as best as we could and placed a new diaper on him, realizing that we had just dumped water into the diaper bag and soaked his last outfit. Handing Alex to Candice, I ducked down behind the car, stripped off my shirt, and put him in my undershirt while I cleaned out his car seat with the rest of the bottle of water, thankful for the scotch guarding on the seat liner that would get me out of this sticky, smelly situation.

~@~

The Elbow Shake

In August 2006 when Alex was about six months old, we traveled to New York to attend Candice's sister Wendy's wedding. No sooner had we arrived at the rehearsal dinner at an old-world, turn-of-the-century restaurant in Little Italy, with lots of atmosphere but few amenities, I took a whiff of a different aroma and instantly knew that I would need to seek out the bathroom. It's one of those smells that you just KNOW without even having to take a peek. So I scooped Alex up.

You never know how much you miss certain things like changing tables that chain restaurants provide until you have to descend a rickety staircase to the only bathroom in the entire establishment. The room was tiny –with barely enough space for the toilet and the sink, complicated by the fact that the door did not latch. I begged the person before me to stand guard while I did the quick change. I was down on the floor, whipping out the changing pad, thinking to myself, "This pad's going to need some sanitizing wipes when we get back to the hotel," and ripped the diaper off. In the split second between diapers, Alex turned into a fountain and started to spray. I threw the old diaper back down but it was too late-it was everywhere—all over him, me, and his only outfit—everywhere.

So I'm on the floor behind the door trying to clean things up as a line of impatient New York patrons was forming outside and pounding on the door, commanding, "Hey, you fall in, in there?" Quickly I put him back together, shoved everything back in the bag, left the room and headed back upstairs-but I had a dilemma: I had put Alex together, but I still had baby pee on my hands. As I ascended the stairs to do the "kid hand off" to Candice, I ran into her mother talking to the groom's sister-in-law, and she insisted on introducing us. The sister-in-law offered her hand. I looked at her, I did the "double-take-errrrr,-stammer," and offered my elbow instead.

The next day at the wedding, I sought the sister-in-law out, if only to assure her that I wasn't really deranged. For the rest of the night, we turned the incident into our own private joke. I wonder, "How many other secret handshakes started with baby pee or other foreign substances on their fingertips?"

Unlike his dad who was secretly mortified over the whole encounter complete with nighttime flashbacks, it didn't faze Alex one bit. He spent the better part of the reception playing peek-a-boo with the flap on his stroller to the amusement of the attendees and the consternation of the best man giving a very elaborate and detailed speech. In spite of all his practice in front of the mirror, he was upstaged by a baby—and how in the world can anyone compete with that?

~@~

A Different Mile High Club

I have one word of advice for prospective parents planning a cross-country trip during the holidays with a toddler under the age of two: DON'T. If you think that the pride of your life is mischievous in his normal surroundings, just wait until you lock him in an aluminum tube with 100 complete strangers for six hours. If the passengers have not banded together and pooled their collective resources to manufacture some tranquilizer darts and duct tape out of drinking straws and the gummy perfume inserts from the in-flight magazines, consider yourself lucky. Over the seat, under the seat, playing with the seatbelt, adjusting the armrest of the person in front of us, standing up on the seats to play with the lights and the stewardess call button. As much as we tried to distract him, he seemed more and more determined to find trouble wherever it was presented.

Just as we were crossing the foothills of the Rocky Mountains somewhere over Utah, he suddenly stopped raising everyone's blood pressure. One by one, the passengers started to breathe a little easier and let the shadow of a smile appear upon their lips. A couple in the row ahead of us even closed their eyes.

Alex's smile was soon replaced with a scowl, as it soon became apparent why he had stopped exploring.

Before I could open my mouth, Candice piped up "You're on duty—take care of your son."

"Bu... Bu...But ... you're closer to the aisle." I protested.

"Doesn't matter. It's your turn to change him," she stated matter-of-factly as I sullenly admitted I had been outdrawn in the diaper changing shootout and shifted around in my seat to extricate myself from the small mountain of blankets, toys, headphones and various other items meant to entertain him on the long journey. I scooped him up and made my way to the back of the plane where two other passengers already waited, dancing from foot to foot impatiently like rock concert attendees during intermission after three light beers.

Finally it was our turn, and the doors creak open and I shuffled inside the room smaller than a coat closet—a closet that suddenly shrank by half when you lowered the changing table. I took a deep breath and closed the door wedging our bodies in a tight space with barely enough room to move my arms. As I attempted to take his shoes off to get to his outfit, Alex reaches over and turns the faucet on full blast, soaking me. I stop the changing and try to get some napkins to wipe up the water, giving Alex the perfect opportunity to disassemble the diaper bag and disgorge all of the contents.

People have told me that having children improves your reflexes – but I had no idea how they were going to be tested at 35,000 feet. One hand darted around collecting the contents not quite as fast as the little hands were pulling them out while the other hand was deftly trying to unsnap the outfit to get to the diaper.

I no sooner get the diaper off, and a voice from the loudspeaker filled me with dread: "ATTENTION PASSENGERS PLEASE RETURN TO YOUR SEATS AND FASTEN YOUR SEATBELTS, WE'RE GOING THROUGH SOME TURBULENCE." the flight attendant noted in a somewhat mirthful tone.

...and as if right on cue, we did. So I'm bouncing around the toilet with a semi-naked baby –with diapers, wipes, butt cream containers and toy cars careening around the toilet along with me, trying to keep the gravity-defying objects, Alex, and my feet from ending up in the dank hole of the flying porta-potty.

Somehow in the middle of all this, I managed to velcro one of the diaper tabs together but the other leg is still swinging free. Alex used the free leg to kick off the diaper. I watched, crestfallen, as it fluttered slowly to the floor, a tiny parachute of white fluttering down into the vinyl canyon, wedging itself behind the toilet.

Resignedly, I started over. As I was fishing around the bag for an unblemished diaper, the rough sky seas parted and the bouncing dropped to a barely discernable jolt. Taking advantage of this lull, and not willing to wait around for it to resume, I slapped the diaper on his butt, velcroed the sides as best I could, scooped up the remaining diaper bag debris and staggered out of the commode.

"Where's his pants?" I was interrogated by Candice upon returning to our seats.

"I changed him—you can re-clothe him." I deadpanned as I thrust our partially-clothed son at my wife.

Brought screechingly down to earth, I resignedly no longer will fantasize about joining the mile-high club. I'm sure I've already become an honorary member and my certificate is in the mail—properly washed and sanitized, of course.

~@~

Jungle Tactics

Every parent has at least one insurmountable, tear-your-hair-out challenge that makes you feel like a complete failure. Often it is caused by our own unrealistic expectations about our children's ability – or inability --to adapt to our pre-conceived timetable. The good news is that in most cases, they survive our ineptitude and manage to become fully contributing members of society in spite of--not because of--us.

My waterloo was potty training. We won the initial battle with the kiddie seat, but those gains were erased as quickly as they had been made. No sooner had we introduced pull-ups and potty seats that it became a full out active resistance kicking and screaming match to get Alex into the bathroom. We'd take him in, and the legs would start running in midair, fists pumping in all directions as we begged and pleaded with him to use the toilet. More often than not, we would put him down and as soon as his feet hit the floor, he'd be sprinting to freedom. We soon learned that the reason you drop the pull-ups to his ankles is to hamper his escape.

Certainly there was no way we were going to make daycare's arbitrary deadline of potty training by age three. As the calendar turned quickly towards the big day, we were at a loss—How in the world would we be ready in time?

I have to credit Candice for fixing this problem—as it seemed well beyond my realm of comprehension to address. She changed tactics. She decided to use our upcoming family cruise vacation (coincidentally over Alex's birthday) as an incentive to help Alex. For three weeks, she prepped Alex every night: "No more zebra diapers when we go on the cruise."

We left for the airport no closer to the goal we had been struggling with for several months, and had brought a suitcase full of diapers, just in case. Candice assured me—"We're going to make this work"—and she was right. Alex walked on board the ship, looked us in the eyes in the cabin and said simply, "No more zebra diapers" and took them off while walking into the bathroom. From that moment on, he never went back. He made up his mind to do it, and he did—in his own time, at his own schedule, and in his own way. Watching myself be proven completely wrong was one of the happiest moments of my parenting life.

But my euphoria proved short-lived. By the last day of the cruise there was a new challenge to overcome—training the child to think about emptying his/her bladder when it's convenient, not when it's urgent.

There is nothing that stops a conversation colder than a little tug on your pant leg accompanied by a little whiney voice saying, "Daddddddddeeeeeeeee, I have to gooooOOoo potttteeeeeeeeeeeeeeeeeeeeeeee," because you know at that very moment you have exactly 3.2 milliseconds to drop everything you are doing and find a bathroom. Your child – who refused to go 20 minutes before when you were in the bathroom with him -- has waited until the very last moment to tell you that he NOW has to pee, as there is not a single ounce that can fit in his turtle-egg sized bladder. You urgently leap up from the table because otherwise, the next sound the entire dining room will hear shouted is, "Daddy IT'S COMING OUT," and a child doing a Michael Jackson imitation trying to hold it all together.

It was lobster night on the boat—the one evening of the cruise where ladies dress in their finest, the men sport their tuxedos or dark suits, and the best menu of the week is on display. We looked forward to this night each cruise, and pre-kids, used to starve ourselves for the day so that there was plenty of room in our stomachs for the feast. On this night, Alex seemed to have "Foodar"—the innate ability to act up 30 seconds before the next course arrived at the table. Our budding three year old would jump from his chair sprinting out of the room, hide under the table tickling our feet, or if he found we weren't paying 100% attention to him, would send butter packets flying across the table, earning him a stern reprimand and a talking to outside the restaurant.

I heard the faint squeak of the kitchen door hinges and the waiter had no sooner put his leg into the dining room with a tray full of dinners that the Foodar kicked in and my new, least favorite phrase was uttered.

"DADDY I have to go POTEEEEEEEEEE." I rolled my eyes.

"Another dinner I'm not going to enjoy," I thought to myself, sighing heavily as I grabbed Alex by the hand I led him to the bathroom located just outside the dining room. I opened the door to the cramped stall barely big enough to fit one person, let alone two, and ushered him inside.

It was nearly impossible to reach around Alex and lift the lid in that tight and claustrophobic space. As I managed to contort my body to raise the seat, Alex leans forward to look in and gets bopped by the seat under his chin. Taken by surprise, he started to cry and as I comforted him looked down and felt a warm spot growing on my leg. I tried to stop it, but I already knew it was too late.

I put him back together and after cleaning myself up as best I could, returned to the table, the savory smells from the plates filled my nostrils partially lifted my mood. I sat and ate in silence, the damp spot where I had washed it out still barely visible on my leg of my dark trousers. Caught between competing thoughts of wanting to eat the lobster and changing my clothes, I opted to grudgingly consume the now lukewarm food. In spite of my outwardly classy appearance, I knew that at that moment, I had become a fire hydrant.

~@~

Overflow

Several months since he gave up the diapers have now passed, and we have adapted to the routine. No longer does he want help. He wants privacy. I dutifully stand guard outside the door, calling in every few minutes, "Are you finished yet?" From the other side of the door I hear him singing on the throne, kicking his legs back and forth and carrying on, and on, and on. First one song, than another, and another—every song he learned that week in school.

"Finished yet?"

"No, I still need more privacy."

"OK. Don't fall in."

"Daddy' you're silly. I can't fall in."

Finally I hear a flush, and a triumphant voice ringing out, "I'mmmmmmmm FINISHED" so I opened the door to help him wash his hands and tidy him back up. I was elated. He did it all by himself.

As I opened the door wider, my elation melted away as I realized that he had unfurled the entire toilet paper roll, shoved it in the bowl and flushed—the waters of the bowl hovering just about an inch below the top.

"Whatever you do, DON'T flush the toilet again," I shouted as I ran to the garage to fetch a plunger and some shop towels.

It took me more plunges than a butter churn to finally clear the blockage. As I stood there with a bead of sweat on my forehead and watched the waters recede, I was confronted with this dilemma: Where do you draw the line between praising the toddler for using the potty all by himself, yet not chastising said child for stuffing an entire roll of toilet paper into the commode?

~@~

6. Sleep... Sleep .... Please Sleeeeeeeeeeep

    Before my son was born, a friend with multiple children of his own pulled me aside and told me, "Sleep while you can, because once the baby is born, you will never sleep again."

    He was right. How right he was, I had no idea until we brought Alex home.

    If you ever wanted to know why your formerly life-of-the-party friends suddenly change from conducting discursive dialog about a wide variety of topics, to answering questions with one word answers, the real reason is, they haven't gotten more than a couple hours sleep a night since their new bundle arrived.

    Babies do not—I repeat, do not—sleep more than two hours straight when they first are born. Every sight, sound, and movement startles them as they get used to their surroundings. After all, they've been in a windowless sack of fluid for the last nine months. Breathing air and seeing light for the first time is pretty foreign stuff to a newborn. As parents of these innocents, you are up when they are up and hope to sleep when they are asleep. The reality is, that when you lay them down for a nap, you spend half the time running around, doing laundry, cleaning up the place, or even taking a shower yourself for the first time in three days. By the time you close your eyes yourself, it's time for the baby to wake up.

Caring for a baby is a vexing, frustrating, tear-what-remains-of- your-hair-out task, coupled with the pride and satisfaction of holding your child in your arms—and one that we would gladly brave all the sleepless nights again to see his first smile.

Now which end does the diaper go on? <<yawn>>

~@~

After six weeks, I had gotten used to the routine. I'd give Alex a bottle and as soon as he was asleep, attempt to get some shut-eye myself, knowing that at least once more overnight, I would be back up feeding and changing him. I thought that if I could minimize disruptions, I could sleep till dawn when Candice took over again. While the plan sounded good in my head; the reality is far different in practice. Oftentimes, I would feed him and sit down in the plush glider to snuggle while I waited for the inevitable diaper change. And that is all I needed: As soon as I sit in that chair, I passed out cold, only to be awoken 20 or 30 minutes later by the warmth spreading in the plastic package nuzzled next to my chest.

Fire Alarm

I had grown to expect the voice, not anticipating that the voice would change so quickly and so suddenly in the course of a day.

I had just fallen asleep and slumber-land took me to that pseudo-dream world when I heard this sound. In my in-between state, I couldn't make sense of it. It sounded …. muffled but urgent. It sounded like a …

FIREALARM

Startled awake, I jump out of bed and start running around, trying to make out where the sound is coming from. In the process I cracked my foot on the bedpost.

ANNNNK! ANNNNNK! ANNNNNNNKKKKKK! ANNNNNNNNKKKKKKKK!

Only it's not coming from the smoke detectors. I check all of the alarms on the floor and NOTHING is going off—yet the shriek is getting louder and louder.

I hobble to Alex's bedroom clutching my throbbing foot already turning blue between my middle toes from the impact. There he lays in his crib, arms and feet pointing flat out like someone knocked the wind out of you.

ANNNNK! ANNNNNK! ANNNNNNNKKKKKK! ANNNNNNNNNKKKKKKKK!

Overnight, his cries had changed from a passive but demanding cry, to a high-decibel, halting, shallow breathed, painfully insistent shriek that sounds remarkably like a house fire alarm. And like a house fire alarm, you have no way of knowing if it is a single candle that wisped a puff of smoke, or the whole house burning down around you. The purpose is to get you to act immediately—and no one can make you drop everything and attend to their needs faster than a baby.

I scooped him up and calmed him down in the glider, my head still throbbing between my ears, and my toe turning more blue and purple by the second, while I contemplated renting him out for the volunteer fire department down the road. I may not get much sleep tonight, but at least I figured out that a father's love can silence the loudest of fire alarms.

~@~

(It Seemed Like a) Hundred Years War

I am a night owl. Ever since I was little, I have always enjoyed staying up late, but heaven help me when it comes time to get up in the morning. I like the cool, quiet of the dark, the time for myself when the rest of the world has gone to bed or has settled in for the evening. I'm just getting started.

I've come to the conclusion, that of all the traits and similarities I share with Alex, the one that I find most dominant is the desire to stay up past our respective bedtimes. The challenges with getting him to sleep when he was little, were nothing compared with the challenges we would experience once he was older, and more mobile.

It started innocently enough. We had moved him to his toddler bed a few weeks before, and he was now able to leave his bed with impunity. I read him a story, tucked him in and turned out the light. Two minutes later, he was up again, running down the hall. I scooped him up and put him back in bed. By the fifteenth or twentieth time we'd played this game (well at least, to him, it was a game; to us it was borderline annoying) the volume started escalating. I regret that I raised my voice but I could not get him to stay in bed and go to sleep. At one point, well over an hour into this dispute, I held his bedroom door closed and demanded that he go back to bed, my authority rapidly diminishing and in desperation, contemplating marching to the garage and finding an extra large roll of duct tape and securing him to the bed frame. Of course, I would never follow through on that—but what parent among us has not at least entertained those thoughts when our child will not listen to us? I now understand what those eye hooks on the outside top of the doors were used for when my brother, sister, and I were little.

Overcome with remorse for even thinking such a horrible thing, I opened the door and went into his room to hold him, brushing the tears off his cheek. I had made him cry. We talked for nearly 15 more minutes about how it was bed time, and that it was time for him to go to sleep. He nodded like he understood. I tucked him in, kissed his forehead, turned out the lights and exited the room.

Not even 20 feet down the hall, I heard the floorboards squeak behind me.

"Get back to bed," I yelled over my shoulder. Alex jumped and hopped back in bed.

There comes a time in every fight between father and son that neither side will give in. I was determined that he would sleep in his own bed that night (else it will be much harder to break the habit later) and he was equally determined to not sleep in his bed that night. I reached the end of the hall and opened and closed the door to our bedroom without actually going in.

Standing in the shadows, I saw movement down the hall as a little ear, and then a tiny eye, and finally a mop of hair peered around the edge of the doorframe. My goal was surprise; His was stealth, as he made his way towards our bedroom door. As he neared the room, I emerged from the shadows. "BACK TO BED," I commanded.

"NO!" Alex defiantly screamed as he dropped himself into a non-violent resistance puddle on the floor making it impossible to pick him up. I bent down and scooped him up, carrying him over the stuffed animals for close to the twenty- seventh time. 'Guess I'm going to be a guard dog tonight,' I thought to myself as I plopped down into the plush glider-rocker on the other side of Alex's room.

As we approached the third hour of this confrontation, I lay down on the floor next to his toddler bed and exhaustedly exhaled the dying breath of a defeated man, "Alex, WHY won't you go to sleep?"

"I'm scared" he said, holding his blanket.

"Why are you scared?" I asked.

"I'm scared of the monsters in the closet," and pointed to the partially opened closet door.

Three --very long and emotionally draining --hours later, I finally understood.

~@~

Outsmarting the Crafty Fox

And so it begins. The opening salvo of the toddler bed wars was the start of trench warfare. Sometimes there would be stealth, other times subterfuge, still others, outright bribery and trickery. He won a few rounds. I won a few rounds. Nightly we squared off with new tactics to send him to bed, and him to escape bed.

I now understand how the warden at Alcatraz felt—although the warden probably never had to sleep next to the inmates to get them to close their eyes. Of course, the moment my eyes drooped, he would deftly crawl over and around me and go downstairs and watch TV. Candice found him one night with the Cartoon Network on. "Where's Daddy?"

"He's asleep in my bed."

"Why are you down here?" she asked, arms resting on her hips.

"Daddy's asleep in my bed," he batted his eyes at her.

Candice carried him back upstairs, sitting him down on my back, waking me up. "Did you lose someone?" she asked.

"Huh?" I responded groggily.

"I found this one down stairs watching TV," as she put him back under the covers. I rolled over to accommodate Alex's return and promptly fell back to sleep. I ended up sleeping in Alex's bed next to him for the remainder of the night—though I woke up the morning with a crick in my neck from the awkward position I slept in and spent the rest of the day with my head cocked at a 45 degree angle – because that was the only position that did not cause me severe pain. At least this time, he actually slept beside me.

Later that week, the old routine started back up again. I put him to bed, and no sooner was I down the hall that I could sense an old west showdown brewing. Standing about eight feet apart we warily eye each other up, our trigger fingers twitching. Him, betting that I won't come back in; me, knowing I should go back in – but that he wins by getting me to bend to his will.

I drew first, moving toward the bed. He sees me commit, and hops back into bed pulling the covers over his face, with only the top portion of his eyes peering out over the blankets. One more time, I tuck him in, and walk out the door, saying, "Now stay there," my voice echoing down the hallway.

Will he stay in bed this time, or will it be one of the nights where he'll hop up more times than a jack-in-the-box? I partially climbed the steps into the darkness to set an ambush. I'd caught him this way before—and the ambush has usually startled him enough to stay in bed for the rest of the night after that.

Crouched down on the stairs, I waited in the shadows. A minute went by. Two minutes. Four minutes. At five minutes, I determined he wasn't going to challenge me tonight and rose to climb the stairs to get on the computer and answer emails.

Forty-five minutes later, I hear giggling downstairs in our bedroom. Descending the stairs to investigate, I peered into our room. There sat Candice and Alex in the overstuffed futon chair with their feet up and watching a TV show.

"What are you doing back up????" I asked. Candice indicated that Alex had opened the door and wandered in, climbing up in the chair next to her.

Just as I had been listening for his footsteps, he had been listening for mine. He waited in silence in his room until I gave up the ambush and climbed the stairs. Only after he heard my heavy footsteps ascend to the upper floor did he stealthily crawl out of bed and tiptoe into our room.

Candice had Alex repeat what he had told her upon entering the room. He nodded knowingly, put his finger to his lips and said, "Sssssssshhhhhhhh. If Daddy hears us giggling, he'll send me back to bed."

In the end, a truce was reached. I would lie down next to him for five minutes each night and he could talk about anything (or nothing) he wanted to talk about. To this day, I still lay down beside him allowing to say whatever is on his mind. These five minutes became the best five minutes of my day.

~@~

Listening Intently

Bed time routine starts with a book. Sometimes it is on the bed, other times it is in the big plush chair. Whenever I find myself nestled in the comfy chair, inevitably I will fall asleep in 5-10 minutes while waiting for him to fall asleep. I end up taking a cat nap for about a half hour before getting up and beginning the second part of my night.

On one night we followed the same routine. I read him stories, he climbed into bed and I flopped into the glider next to him and within minutes was out cold. I woke up with a jolt a few minutes later to see that he had turned on his fish tank light, rolled over and uncovered his stash of books that he had carefully hidden in the corner of his bed. He sat up in his bed, pulled little Elmo into his lap, and started to read.

Alex told Elmo the story of the train, how the train was fast, and that when the train went into the tunnel, he turned on a big light so Elmo could see.

I held my eyes closed and carefully listened to the story, taking in every syllable and inflection. It was short by adult standards, but long for a two- and-a-half-year old—and in five minutes he was done. I heard the book snap shut and he tucked Elmo in next to him as he slowly drifted off to sleep. I waited there another fifteen minutes until I was sure he was out cold.

He never knew that night that he had a second attentive listener. He never knew how much joy I felt listening to him tell the story. I didn't want to interrupt him, so I quietly slipped away, the memory of his storytelling etched so brilliantly in my mind.

~@~

Pajama Climber

From deep in my sleep, I hear the sound of a cat clawing at the carpet. What cat? We don't have a cat. Ever since college, I've been allergic to them. The sound shuffles in the hallway, closer to the room. 'Go ahead and gobble me up,' I thought in my dream-like state, 'I'm not moving from these covers.' I hear a slight creak of the floorboard at the entrance to our bedroom and can sense something there. Something breathing, something looking out into the darkness, something small and shadowy in form as it makes its way over to the window.

I feel the little air wave ripples in the still of the night and the warmth of his body as he makes his way along the windowsills until it is standing over me, dragging the decorative pillows on the floor behind him into a pile. I open my eyes slightly just as the shadowy figure grabs hold of my pajama sleeve and starts to pull himself up into the bed like a mountain climber scaling the Matterhorn. I start to roll over from the new weight being applied to myself, the human rope. Quick as a wink, he's nestled between us, and with a final kick and a push in the back, I capsize, arms flailing in slow motion to regain support, and tumbling off the bed onto the decorative pillows below.

I had been evicted—not by a cat, but by a child in a dinosaur bunny suit.

~@~

Little Lightning Bolts

The new game we learned has a bit of a dark side—in that it taught Alex the art of the magician's static charge. I was about nine years old when I had learned it at my Aunt Nancy's wedding, and used it to torment several older cousins and a stray photographer or two. It kept all of us occupied for the night, but now they are avenged.

Shuffle... Shuffle... Shuffle

I hear the footsteps enter the darkened room again from deep inside my slumber. This has become a routine occurrence over the last few nights. I know we have a pint-sized visitor as I patiently wait for him to come near so I can snap my eyes awake and startle him into scrambling back to his room without me having to leave the warm bed.

Shuffle... Shuffle... Shuffle

I can sense a presence in the room inching closer and closer to me. Candice stirs slightly—she can sense him too, but chooses to ignore him. Nighttime is a father's responsibility.

Shuffle... Shuffle...Shuffle

I half open a single eye, and vaguely make out the shadows on the wall. Each movement recorded in the nascent pre-dawn light, but my eyes grow heavy again and close tight.

Shuffle... Shuffle... Shuffle

I can detect a slight change in temperature as he comes up stealthily upon me—his eyes piercing the darkness. He stands transfixed, a few inches from my head, a demon in pint-sized form.

Shuffle ... Shuffle... Shuffle

He leans in on me to touch my face.

KA-POW!!!

The static charge-- a mighty lightning bolt worthy of Zeus, the king of the gods –leapt from his fingers. My skin scorched and I startled instantly awake, howling in pain.

I levitated vertically a good six inches above the bed for a split second before the covers that surrounded me yanked me back to the mattress with the resounding snap of a fighter pilot making a carrier landing. I heard the quilting make the sound of a quiet exhale of a slow rushing balloon as all of the pieces one by one fell back down upon the bed.

"I'm thirsty," I hear a little voice exclaim.

The faint smell of my own smoking flesh wisped up in the air filling my nostrils, the pain in my cheek dulling by the moment, and my sleepy body jolted permanently awake in those pre-dawn hours as I untangled myself from my covers. Holding my jaw where the spark had struck, I trudged down stairs to retrieve a glass of water for the magician in training. Perhaps when morning breaks, maybe I'll teach him that water shorts out electricity.

~@~

7. Don't Leave Dad Alone with Kid

Picture a three-foot tall toy top, or a Tasmanian Devil, wound up and released at full speed. It careens off the walls, knocks over plates, scares the dog, spills a glass of milk, all the while spinning and ebbing against the wall with a crayon. As a father of a toddler, once your child is mobile, you are always playing defense, three steps behind, catching the plate as it falls, intercepting the cup as it wobbles before toppling over. You can't take your eyes off of your darling for a second, because you never know from which direction the next attack is coming from.

Soldiers call this crippling fear of the next attack 'Post Traumatic Stress Disorder.' Parents call it 'Presence of Toddler Stress Disorganizer.' Either way, the causes and symptoms are the same: Crying out in the middle of the night, heart racing, sweating, reliving the moment earlier that day that you dove a millisecond too late to save your wife's favorite crystal bowl from shattering into million pieces while you re-rolled the entire roll of toilet paper that had been unrolled in the bathroom, that happened when you were mopping up the milk jug that had been tipped over trying to pour milk into the bowl of Cheerios.

Not that the crystal bowl should have been left out on that side table that the child could find, much less knock over; but regardless, you are on duty, so you're the one who gets yelled at when Mom comes back from the store. When the roles are reversed, Mom NEVER has any of these problems—or if she does, you never hear about it-- because whatever was broken has been fixed before you get home, hidden away in hopes that you don't notice the casualty, or displayed prominently on the dining room table as a lesson to Dad as to why to not leave his prized alcohol bottle shaped like a Tiki god that he's had since college where the child can reach it. (Come to think of it, just how *DID* that bottle manage to fall off the third shelf?)

I've also come to the conclusion that long ago when the world was young, children learned to stop time. Adults and older children have since lost that ability, except in moments of extreme utter self-mortification when time cannot seem to move fast enough. It's a skill that disappears when we get to the age of five - and most likely the reason that kids are always asking how much time has elapsed. You see—to them—days have gone by, and for us, it's a blink of an eye, a blur in the cosmos.

It seems that the secret of this skill is chaos—the power that disrupts the normal routine just long enough for the fates to stop everything freeze-frame to move the chairs around, sit back and let the fun and games begin. The next time the phone rings, or the dog barks, or dinner goes up in a ball of flame, look around and notice where the child is. I guarantee you he/ she won't be in that spot when you get back.

Alex was contentedly sitting on the futon thoroughly enjoying watching cartoons when the phone rang. I walked across the room to answer it—"a telemarketer," I huffed. Turning around, Alex had vanished. I glanced down the hall and he was seated on a stool and holding a small red bottle. Somehow, he had teleported past me to the bathroom, gotten up on the stool, opened the nail polish and had proceeded to paint his toes a bright, loud, fire-engine red, like he had seen Mommy do a hundred times. Alex improved upon Mom's handiwork by painting most of the toes on his foot, not just the toenails that help Mom look so pretty.

I rushed down the hall. He saw me immediately and hopped off the chair. Dodging and weaving, I chased him in circles around the bathroom –attempting to block his escape and preventing the red-footed urchin from leaving a seemingly bloody, but glazed and shiny trail through the bedroom. He parried by using the stool as a bumper, staying on the opposite side of me, zigging while I zagged until I lunged over the stool—which of course my foot caught the wheels on the bottom sending me crashing down on top of it zipping in the other direction while he red-footed it to freedom.

I caught him just as he was about to run down the hall on the carpet, though not before planting enough footprints on the tile bathroom floor to fill out an Arthur Murray dance card. I cleaned up his foot, in spite of his protests – but left the toenails painted. It was a small victory for him – but at least it's one that kept him quiet while I scrubbed the tile floor with nail polish remover.

The next day a friend of his brought over some removable tattoos, which were promptly affixed to both of their arms. I think I detected a new swagger in his step as this two-and-a-half- year old – with tattooed arms sticking out of a "muscle shirt" and red painted toenails stomping around the kitchen. Lucky for me, it was a phase he outgrew by the weekend. I wasn't willing to explain this profound turn of events to daycare come Monday.

~@~

Track Star

From the moment Alex took his first steps, Alex has been a sprinter. On his first birthday, what started as a slow lumbering gait across the room to his baby girlfriend, turned into a full-fledged sprint and he hasn't stopped since. Keeping after him is a built in weight loss program. I might as well have hired him as a pint-sized fitness instructor—one like my days in high school gym class with those horrible polyester shorts and double sided shirts—who, on the spur of the moment will send me on a "suicide drill" running from one line to the next, touching the line and sprinting back to where I started in the shortest amount of time possible.

Recently Alex has given me ample opportunity to practice those maneuvers. One day while paying for some groceries at the market, he inched his way out and in front of me and took off running to the door. In the time it took me to swipe my card, Alex had gotten around me and made it $\frac{3}{4}$ of the way to the automatic doors – well over 75 feet away. I dropped the groceries I was bagging on the counter, turned and sprinted for the door—just catching him before he made it outside. I scooped him up and raced back to the cash register, and with him in a one-arm bear hug, signed the receipt with the free hand.

The next weekend, we visited Fredrick, MD and strolled along the canal. Hand in hand with Candice and Alex by our side, I turned to ask her a question. She had answered about half of the question when she stops mid-sentence shouting, "GET ALEX!"

I wheeled around, and the little boy who was just standing next to me a moment ago, had opened up a 25 yard gap between us and was running full tilt towards the bend in the canal ahead. It took me a full-out sprint of nearly the entire length of a football field before I closed the distance and intercepted him—less than a few feet before both of us would have fallen into the stream.

As any parent can attest, the unexpected plunge into an algae filled canal will ruin just about anybody's well-intentioned romantic walk. A few seconds more, and I would have become the creature from the putrid lagoon, much to the grins of the onlookers—at least one of whom probably has a camera that I will find the video uploaded on the internet.

~@~

The Streaker

A couple thousand years ago, the first Olympians competed wearing not a stitch of clothing. Part of it was to honor the gods, the other part of it, I'm sure, was to make sure that no warrior from antagonistic city states was hiding a weapon.

I'm convinced there's yet another reason. Nakedness makes you run faster.

Want to know how I know this? Have you ever tried to catch a two-year old fresh out of the tub before you can get him dressed? You towel him off and BAM-- as soon as you've removed the drying cloth, he takes off running. Before you can blink an eye, he's all the way down the hall, rounding the corner, and sprinting to freedom.

I can't tell you how many times I've had to leap off the tile floor and chase him down. Sometimes he'll get all the way to the stairs before I can catch the naked toddler. Other times he'll circle the ottoman keeping it between us – until I get frustrated and lunge at him, usually tripping over it in the process.

On rare occasions, I'll actually catch him and take him to his room—the naked running man churning his feet in mid air. Only when I clamp a diaper on him does he lose his magical speed ability and settle down.

...and I'm guessing that's the real reason streakers run so fast.

~@~

Three-and-a-Half Minutes

Three-and- a-half minutes is a very long amount of time. A world-class sprinter can run a mile in three and a half minutes. A car traveling at highway speeds can cover over almost four miles – and a nearly three-year-old can get himself into all kinds of trouble when left out of eyesight for that period of time.

Alex was playing with his train set when I heard the phone ring. I watched him out of the corner of my eye innocently moving the cars around the track as I raced across the room to the phone. Along the way, I passed the clock on the wall reading in big bold letters: 3:28. I remember the time because I was wondering to myself when Mom was coming home to relieve me—she was taking her time coming back from the store. I reached the phone and answered it—it was a friend of Candice's Dad calling for an update on his deteriorating medical condition. I filled him in on the details we knew from seeing him earlier that day, that the brain cancer had rapidly developed and was causing a series of strokes leaving him paralyzed in bed. I answered his friend of many years the questions he desperately needed answered, momentarily forgetting about my child care responsibilities. We said our good-byes; I hung up the phone and crossed the room again in front of the clock. 3:31 it read.

Where was Alex? He wasn't by the trains where I had left him. He wasn't in the bathroom, and I finally heard him shuffling around in my office. Turning the corner, I saw him climb down off the chair and hand me a book.

"I drew you picture," he said, eyes beaming.

I looked down and he had found his Aunt Wendie's wedding album in a delicate paper mâché cover with pressed flowers, and had taken a blue magic marker and had drawn a picture on the cover. I looked up, and saw that the computer had gone into the black screen of death (which is worse than the blue screen of death one sometimes sees).

"What happened here?" I inquired forcefully with a disbelieving, blinking gaze that mimicked the DOS prompt cursor on the screen. There was no graphical interface. When I had left the computer a few minutes ago, the computer was fully operational. Now it blinked bleakly, my opaque, hollowed-out reflection staring back at me in the dimness of the darkened screen.

"I played a game." Alex said, pointing at the monitor.

It had been... exactly three-and-a-half minutes.

~@~

Pay Attention to Me

Most toddlers have short attention spans. Anything longer than 5-10 minutes and they begin to grow bored and start searching for something else to do. (In today's media-saturated environment, many adults are too.) There are reasons children's books only have 20-30 words on a page. By the time you reach the end of the page, they want to turn to the next one.

I try to vary the tone and inflection. OFTEN my ReADings sOUNd A liTTle disJOINTed in my attempt to keep Alex's attention. In spite of that, there have been plenty of times that he has gotten up in the middle of a story and simply walked out of the room. I know he isn't doing it on purpose, and that I should let it slide off my back, but I find myself getting uncontrollably irritated and wanting to strap him in the chair till I am done reading the story to him. I've barked, more like an old harmless toothless hound dog than a Doberman Pincher, "Hey, if you walk away from me, we're not going to finish the story," as he turns the corner and wanders out of the room, or over to the bookshelf to pick out another book.

Lately though, he's wanted to read the stories to me. Though he can't yet read, he makes up stories based on the pictures. And just to make sure I'm listening to him, will grab my face in his hands, smush my cheeks together, look me in the eye and say, "Pay attention to me. I'm not reading this story until you listen. Now pay attention to me."

~@~

I am not Paul Stankus

As every parent knows from their own childhood, there are escalating levels of a request from Mom or

Dad. It starts with an informal request using the nickname, and then progresses to the real name. If you still aren't listening, it becomes your full first name—and finally just before you are about to get smacked, you hear the rumbling of 'PAUL ALAN STANKUS get your butt over here NOW!'

At that point, you have two options—you fall quickly in line, or you hope that you can outrun Mom and Dad because they have reached the point of no return.

I can attest to the fact that I had heard my full name uttered on more than one occasion as a child as I was usually into some kind of mischief—overflowing the sink to watch the waterfall form, digging up the bottom of the driveway to provide a lagoon for my toy boats, etc. - though I quickly learned that there were few things worse than defying either the wrath of Mom or Dad. One doesn't easily forget those tongue-lashings. As a parent, I've found myself repeating the same patterns as my own parents. I may let a few more things slide, but Alex still has figured out my fault lines and will carefully stride right up to the line without going over, daring me to cross it to provoke a reaction.

Candice was in the kitchen one day and asked Alex to help with some dishes. It was a simple request, one in keeping with teaching a toddler household responsibility.

"Sparky, can you take your cup to the sink?" Candice said from behind the countertop. It was a name she called him since birth because he only had two switches, on and off, like a spark plug.

(silence)

"Sparky, can you please take your cup to the sink?"

(silence)

Apparently at age three, kids become deaf.

"Alex, Mommy asked you to take your cup to the sink," I interject. "Please take your cup to the sink."

(silence)

"Alexander. Please take your cup to the sink."

"No."

"Alexander, I ASKED you to take your cup to the sink."

(silence)

"Alexander, this is your last chance. Put your cup in the sink."

"OooooKaaaaaaaaaay." (Alex moves the cup from the table to the couch arm.)

"PUT THE CUP IN THE SINK!"

(Alex dumps the cup over intentionally on the couch)

"ALEXANDER PAUL STANKUS PUT THAT CUP IN THE SINK NOW!!" I shouted at the top of my lungs.

"I'm NOT Paul Stankus... YOU ARE."

I could feel my blood boiling inside of me. If I had talked that way to my parents, I surely would have gotten a wooden spoon swiftly across my rear. I looked at Candice with a growl and a grimace, nose starting to narrow and shudder, snorting like a bull straining at the paddocks. She responded with a snort and a suppressed giggle, eyes bulging out of her head as she fought back an uncontrollable laugh. I shot her laser dagger eyes, which only succeeded in scorching the last semblance of decorum remaining in the room. Unable to suppress it any longer, she shuffled quickly out of the kitchen, the sounds of her stockings making a shoosh-shoosh-shoosh across the floor like a leaky water balloon—its sounds mimicking my rapidly vanishing authority with my son.

~@~

Diary of the Getting Ready For School

I have to give Candice credit—she knows how to get an unruly bunch out the door. Part justice, judge, and jury and part sheep-herder—when Candice is in charge of logistics we can march out the door in record time. When I am in charge—not so much. I guess I just don't have the timetable instinct honed to a razor-sharp edge.

One morning, we flipped schedules so Candice could get to an early film shoot, which left me in charge of getting a sleepy toddler out the door. It seems that this day, like any day the substitute teacher is at the front of the classroom, that all of the shenanigans had been stored up to spring on me at once—a jack-in-the-box ready to reach out and twit me on the nose.

Here's how my day went:

> 6:30 AM alarm goes off. SLAM! Snooze. I roll over and go back to sleep.
>
> 6:39 AM alarm goes off. SLAM! Snooze. Back to sleep.
>
> 6:48 AM alarm goes off. 'Oh all right, I'm up now.'

Stagger- stager-stagger down hall—my eyes are still slits seeing the first rays of sunlight peaking through the rooftops outside my window.

Splash water in my face. What was that thing I was supposed to do this morning?

More splashing water. Time to turn on the shower.

Oh wait--- I can't do that yet—Candice wanted me to give Alex a bath.

The heck with the bath- I'll take Alex in the shower with me- that'll save time.

Plod down hall—to Alex's room—Alex is sound asleep.

I gently nudge him—he shrugs me off.

I nudge him again—and he stirs and shrugs me off.

I turn on the light and he grabs the blanket and covers his head (gee, I wonder where he gets it from?)

I scoop him up and take him in the other room, he winces in protest.

OK where's his clothes?

Shuffle through drawers.

Here's a shirt. And pants. Where are the socks - these don't match.

Walk back to bedroom. Alex is asleep again.

Must determinedly undress semi-sleeping child—who's unconsciously kicking forcefully to not get out of his bunny suit.

Finally undressed—I carry him into bathroom.

Now the challenge - how do I get myself undressed while holding a naked, squirming, sleepy toddler without dropping him.

Standing on the edge of my pajamas, I managed to walk them backwards. Shifting Alex back and forth in my arms, I wiggle out. He's just starting to awake.

Shower's ready. I carry him in and begin to wash him off.

I no sooner get him lathered up, when he finally wakes up for good, and in the process, kicks me in the groin. I'm doing my best to keep him in my arms without dropping him as I readjust, using the corner as a propping limb.

At that moment, he reaches back and turns the hot water on full force.

'Yeeeeeeeeeeow!'

Miraculously I did not drop him, finished the shower and put him on the foot towel. No sooner did I put him down, that he took off like a shot, still dripping water all over the place.

I chase after him, hitting the water-soaked floor and skid across the tiles into the doorframe, nearly tearing the door from its hinges as I attempted to steady myself. Alex is already down the hall and around the corner.

Chase Alex around the ottoman a dozen times. I finally lunge at him across the ottoman and catch him, carrying him to his bedroom to get his clothes and wedging him between my legs to keep him from running away. I think I saw this move in a rodeo or a bullfight once.

I carried Alex downstairs, turn on cartoons, throw bagel in toaster, run back upstairs to get changed myself. I manage to get my shirt and pants on before Alex very loudly calls out 'JUICE PLEASE.'

I heard the toaster ding and run back downstairs. In those few moments in between, he has managed to grind the Philadelphia Cream Cheese into the rug and empty an entire box of straws on the floor.

I picked up the straws from the floor, shove the bagel in his hands, run back upstairs, and get one sock on before I hear Alex yelp. I run back down the stairs to find that he has crawled up on the couch, transited over to the kitchen countertop, and turned the faucet on full blast, soaking himself.

I cleaned him up as best I can, only to find that there is no lunch made. Worse yet, there is no lunch meat—so I cobble together a variety of snacks and a cheese sandwich.

Scooping Alex up, we run back upstairs, stopping only briefly in my room to finish putting on my sock and shoes. Meanwhile I'm stripping the kid for the second time this morning, while trying in vain to reason with him that no, he can't wear his sopping wet Thomas shirt because it is 35 degrees out. He pulls out every trick in the book to keep his wet shirt on, and I resort to several wrestling moves to extricate him from his favorite shirt. Finally re-dressed, I carry him downstairs, throw on his winter jacket, and head for the door.

We forgot something for school. I unlock the door, go back inside to retrieve it. In the 5 seconds we are back inside, Alex takes off the jacket and runs around the island again. I put him back together – I lock the door, set the alarm and we walk briskly to school.

No time for chitchat, I drop Alex off and sprint out of the building, only to see the bus already at the bus stop leaving me behind in a trail of dust. Running full throttle, with a knapsack, a brief case and a lunch bag after the bus, it brought back memories of my own childhood when I was always late for the bus. Huffing and puffing I caught the bus three blocks later, only because it had to stop and wait for the traffic light.

I get off the bus, enter the metro station platform, flop into a seat and by the time we got to the second stop, I was sound asleep on my way to work.

Of course, for my final *coup de grâce*, I overslept my destination, and woke up at Judiciary Square metro, four stations beyond my own, and had to take another train back in the opposite direction to start my day at the office.

This was probably the day I should have hit the buzzer in the morning, admitted defeat, and promptly pulled the covers over my eyes. Of course, hindsight is always 20/20 when you are taking the train back in the other direction to get to the place you should have been going to in the first place.

~@~

8. Collisions Between Work and Life

Men don't multi-task. We work best when we focus linearly on one thing, and then when completed (or at least when we say its completed—which may or may not be completed to the satisfaction of the woman in the room) we then move on to the next item on our list. Women, on the other hand, are very good at balancing multiple, competing projects all at the same time. This is why nature intended women to be the primary caregivers. They can keep three children from painting the dog polka dots with the permanent marker from the drawer, while chatting with their girlfriends and making dinner for the family. Men—not so much. We focus first on the child, taking the marker away, but not replacing it with something else to occupy his time—resulting in large screaming tantrums, turn back to the stove that is now boiling over because we didn't think to turn down the heat to go deal with the child, and completely forgetting about both when either the phone rings or we spy something on the television. So instead of a carefully balanced choreography of a mother's household, when a man is in charge, disordered chaos reigns supreme.

When you add work responsibilities to this, our carefully thought-out plans fall apart like a house of cards.

As fathers, we know our primary responsibility is to put food on the table. We go to work each day to earn money for our family to live. We are very focused on what we do during the work day, because without that paycheck, the family would soon be living out of a cardboard box under a railroad bridge. We take our responsibilities seriously and while we may secretly wish to be cliff divers in Acapulco, running with the bulls in Pamplona, or some other profession equally exciting and dangerous, we make sacrifices for our wife and children.

I work in an industry that is very generous with its flexible work schedule. If I need to work from home for a family issue or medical appointment, I can work from home. Candice works in a profession requiring her to be on-site to do her job—as it is hard to create television commercials from the comfort of our own couch. Consequently, when Alex gets the latest bug from daycare, (affectionately known as 'the land of little people with big germs') I am usually the one who stays home with him. In spite of Candice's near obsession with hand washing and sanitizer, I'm home with him about once a month, sometimes more.

No matter what people say, it is very challenging to work a full day, at the same time as caring for a little one nasally and insistently shouting 'TISSUE!'

One morning Candice needed to go to the office early—so I was in charge of drop-off and pick-up at daycare and arranged to work from home. I had a conference call at 9 AM, so I figured I could easily drop him off, run back to the house, and be on the call in enough time to get done what I needed to do. I hadn't counted on the fact that my son—who is normally an early riser-- was still sound asleep at 7:30 AM, still asleep at 8:00, and, in spite of my persistent nudging, passed out cold at 8:30 and 9:00 AM.

Knowing that he was still asleep, I fixed his breakfast of a waffle and sippy cup of milk, and went back to preparing for the conference call. Sure enough, 5 minutes into the call, the slumbering giant awoke, with loud plaintive cries that needed attending to. I pulled him out of the crib, dragged him downstairs gave him his waffle and went back to the call. Standing on the other side of the house, I could plainly see Alex—and he could see me. I thought -- incorrectly it turns out—that I was on mute.

Alex saw me across the room, picked himself up off the floor and walked to me, waffle and milk in his hand, calling out "waffle, waffle, waffle" and chased me around the room in a figure-8 pattern. I'd go to one side of the room, and he'd follow this carefully choreographed dance for upwards of 15 minutes, repeating "waffle" the whole time. Finally he stopped by the kitchen counter. In the loudest voice he could possibly manage, he blurted out "GRAPES PLEASE." It was loud enough that the entire conference call burst out laughing.

"I'm not on mute?" I asked chagrinned into the phone.

"No," came the multiple laughter-stiffled replies.

The jig was up—they had been listening to the full transcript of my conversations—which were apparently much more entertaining than the contents of the conference call itself.

~@~

Toddler Tech Support

One night I had brought some work home from the office, and had set up the laptop in the living room. While typing away, Alex saw me and toddled over to the couch. Instinctively, he started banging away on the keyboard—because that is exactly what daddy was doing.

All of a sudden, I hear a mechanized voice emanating from the monitor.

T...H..E C..O..M..P..U..T..E..R..
S..T..A..R..T..E..D R..E..A..D..I..N..G
T..H..E D..O..C..U..M..E..N..T O..N
T..H..E...S..C..R..E..E..N.

And I couldn't turn it off. Try as I may, the laptop kept reading the words on the screen out loud. I finally had to reboot the machine to turn off the audio reader.

The next day I asked our IT department how to turn on the audio screen reader. Their response:

"What screen reader????"

I immediately offered them the services of my one-year-old, who apparently knows more about computers than they do.

~@~

Conference Call Redux

Home again with a sniffly Alex and lucky that I can work from home while keeping an eye on him. I would have taken some sick time to focus exclusively on him, but as luck would have it, I had multiple conference calls stacked and racked that I was expected to participate in—so the old standby - the electronic baby sitter known as the DVD player will have to suffice while I attend to my work calls.

I set him up in the family room down the hall from my office—I can keep an eye on him, yet still get some work done. In order to make your escape, you turn on the video about 10 minutes before you need to skedaddle—so that by the time you need to depart, he is fully engrossed in the movie and doesn't notice you walking down the hall. Alex, however, notices everything. As I dial into the call, I hear him shuffling down the corridor. Just as I am announcing myself on the call, Alex very loudly shouts out, "Daddy, clean my boogies." I listen as the conference call service announces to the rest of the attendees, "Paul (and in a tiny background voice, "Clean my boogies"). My co-workers stifled a snort.

Not exactly the way I wanted to start off the call.

I wiped his nose. The call started. I waited for the leader of the call to finish talking so I could give my update.

As I began talking, I see this little hand swinging toward me in what felt like slow motion. I think I got out the words, "I'd like to update everybody on..." before **WHAM!**

His hand connected right between my legs, sending my voice a couple of octaves higher.

Gasping for breath, choking back the tears and trying desperately to retain all sense of professional decorum, I blurt out in a strained voice, could the next person give their update, I'm working from home with a sick child and there's a matter I must attend to.

I fumbled for the mute button-- hoping that I actually turned it on this time-- before I let out a painful, silenced howl.

That'll teach me to put work before the needs of a sick child.

Later that same day, I had a follow-up call scheduled. This time, the conference call coincided with Alex's nap—so I wasn't taking any chances—into the crib he went. He usually cries for a few moments and then settles himself down to sleep. I heard him in the crib rattling the bars and protesting loudly, but there was no way I was going to let him interrupt a second call that day—particularly since most of the people on the first call were also scheduled to be present on the second call. So I ignored him, confident that he would go to sleep on his own like he usually does.

I dialed in, and was just getting ready to speak again, when I hear some shuffling on the steps.

"That's odd... We're the only ones here," I thought and went back to preparing to speak. Just then a little mop haired boy comes up the stairs and says to me sweetly, "All done sleeping. Play now."

Now, I'm certain that he was in the crib when I left him 10 minutes earlier. I'm also certain that he is currently standing up looking at me, no longer in his crib. I further know that he has never yet crawled out of his crib—so I sit there puzzled. "How did he get up the stairs????"

Luckily on this second call I only had a little bit to say, so I said my part, and logged off, taking him down to his crib again. I placed him back in and turned to walk away. Over my shoulder I peered to get a glimpse of how he escaped.

In less than a minute after me putting him in the crib, he had maneuvered to the corner, thrown his leg over the front railing, placed his other hand on the side rail, and flipped his second leg over. Then, with cat-burglar like reflexes, he shimmied down the side of the crib. He turned around and saw me standing there. As he looked at me and I looked at him caught in the act, I saw him try to climb back up, chagrinned, as if to say—"I'll be back here in my crib if anyone needs me."

I put him back in three more times—and each time he escaped again. By the final time, he had gotten his escape down to 30 seconds or less, I knew that his days in the crib are over, and that I had a new task to do that evening when Candice came home—reconfiguring the crib into the toddler bed.

Since it seems that he wasn't going to sleep in the crib, that he was more intent on escaping, and I couldn't stand there in his room watching him the whole time, I scooped him up and took him back to the room where his toys are so I could keep an eye on him as I worked.

~@~

I love the days when Candice and I switch schedules on daycare duties. I'd much rather be dropping off and work later than to come in early and rush to pick up. Unfortunately, our schedules work out such that it is usually the other way around. Still, I enjoy when I get to sleep in a little longer and leisurely get to daycare before making my way to work.

Alex and I arrived at daycare, and the provider and I exchanged pleasantries. As I turned to leave, I feel two small hands on my thighs. I glanced down and Alex looks up at me saying "Sit Back Daddy. No go work."

So I dutifully sat down and chatted with the other parents.

For the next 15 minutes, every time I tried to get back up, Alex would come back over to me saying, "Sit Back," and push me back hard against the seat. I was a virtual prisoner.

Once I succeeded in standing up – only to be pushed back harder than ever. I lost my balance and crumbled back into my seat. He climbs up on the couch next to me, looks me in the eyes grabs both of my cheeks with his two hands and says "Look at me. Look at me. Sit back."

I finally left daycare and got to work, arriving several minutes late. As I tried to sneak in, my boss turns the corner and says, "A little late today huh?"

"Sorry boss, I was being held captive by my two-year-old son."

~@~

9. Day Care Misadventures

Daycare. Probably one of the most important decisions a working parent can make—who will watch your child while you are at work. It is a bit disheartening that complete strangers will see your cherub more than you, but that is the fact of life when you are a dual-income family. The lucky parents are the ones with family nearby, individuals you (mostly) trust and have grown up with. The rest of us fend for ourselves with a variety of daycare—both in-home, and more formal schooling arrangements.

I mentioned earlier that our first attempt at daycare did not turn out so well, as our space on the waiting list we had reserved nine months earlier wasn't ready in time. We turned to our second daycare out of the desperation of needing to find a new place within two weeks, only to find out in December that the woman watching Alex was returning to China in January. We interviewed nannies, but were shocked back into reality when one of them wanted the equivalent of half of one of our pay, two weeks paid vacation, a car at her disposal, and a 401k—which reality-checked us into what we could actually afford. Luckily on our third try, we found an at-home daycare run by a very loving woman named Miss Jane, a former high school vice-principal from her native Pakistan, and her daughters who gave Alex the nurturing and affection he needed to thrive and emerge as a person. Under her expert tutelage, we watched Alex develop his usually quiet, often brooding, decisive child with a sense of social justice that I have come to know and love.

Even as a small child, Alex knew when he was wronged. Being one of the younger children in the daycare, he often was at the mercy of older boys and girls—and though the daycare providers intervened to prevent fights and screaming matches from starting up, there is only so much you can do when it's one toddler against the equivalent of five older siblings, none of which have yet learned to share. Rarely, if ever, does he complain – he just goes off and does his own thing. However when he wants to make a statement, he can do it in dramatic fashion.

One day in early spring, Alex was playing outside with a toy – and a bigger kid wanted the toy that Alex had in his hand, so he lumbered over, bit Alex on the arm, and took the toy from him. Alex cried out as one would expect, and appealed to the caregiver for intervention. She leaned over, picked him up, held him for a few moments and put him back down on the ground. Not entirely satisfied with the results, Alex went back to the corner where the older kid was playing with the contraband toy.

Instead of getting into a shoving match and taking the toy back by brute strength, he reached out to the water spigot, turned the water on full force, and drenched the big kid.

The older kid bellowed as the water ran down his shirt and into his pants, pooling in the cuffs of the jeans, sloshing over the edge like a waterfall. As the daycare owner ran over to turn off the water, Alex simply walked-skipped away --the look on his face said "wasn't me, I have no idea what you are talking about," --the angelic halo held up by the devil horns hidden in his red hair.

This kid doesn't get mad, he gets even. The big kid hasn't touched him since.

~@~

A Spirited Defense

Alex is generally very well behaved at school. I think I can count on one hand the number of times in almost two years that Miss Jane had pulled me aside and informed me of a problem.

Today was one of those days.

I walked in the door at my normal pick up time, and was met by the stern gaze of the former Assistant Principal. "We had an altercation today," she announced in the same voice she'd probably used hundreds of times years ago uttering the word all kids fear -- DETENTION.

Around the corner, Alex peered out partially from behind the wall. He KNEW we were talking about him. I stooped down to his eye level and asked him what happened—but was not prepared for his response.

Alex began to tell me a story that he and another boy wanted the same toy. Alex had the toy, the older boy took it, and Alex, not about to let it go, pulled it back—resulting in a tearful, terse, tug of war that Miss Jane had to separate.

I listened to the story, conflicted. I wanted to say I was proud of him for fighting back – to not let the older boy push him around, for standing his ground. I also wanted to say to him that fighting isn't the answer and to share the toys. How do you choose one right way over the other – when nuance is lost on a two-year-old?

In the end I chose compromise over conflict. I encouraged him to share his toys –all the while secretly longing to give him a high-five for standing up to a bully and tell him how proud I was of his courage—though I doubt Miss Jane would have approved.

~@~

Projected Shame

Later that year, as the weather turned from summer to fall, the daycare children took as much advantage of the outdoors as they could possibly handle. As school started, a young man in his late teens moved in next door-- very urban, very hip, and very into his own coolness factor. Every day, he completely ignored the little kids next door as he turned the rap music up loud and dragged on his cigarette. Miss Jane watched him like a hawk, making sure that no stray butts wandered into the children's play area. (I'm sure that words were spoken between the two in off-hours, but during the day, there was a feeling of a brokered cease-fire and an uneasy détente.)

Alex picked up on the friction between the two. One day he decided to take matters into his own hands as he marched from the play area over the man's patio and stood in front of him pointing a stern, wagging finger. In his loudest voice possible, he shouts out, "EEEEEEEWWWW... YUCKY."

The man removed the cigarette from his mouth and held it in midair, the smoke tendrils wisping in the air like a spirit escaping.

Alex again pointed at the cigarette and repeated his statement. "EEEEEEEWWWWW... YUCKY."

The young man took one last drag of the cigarette, tossed it to the ground, and stomped on it in disgust before quickly turning around and retreating in a huff to the confines of his house.

Alex solved the problem in a way that only a toddler could: Shame-- Forceful, and direct, with no subtleties. For the remainder of the fall and winter, the man gave the daycare children their space and retreated to the side of the house away from the disapproving eyes of a little child defending his play area. He had been shamed by his actions.

The Question

All parents fear "the question" – and I don't even need to tell you "The question" because ever since your own adolescence, you have been preparing for the moment to describe to your own kids the answers to the question. And until it happens, you have this foreboding lingering unanswered question lurking in the back of your mind.

And it all depends on the age—if they're little, we fib to our children and say the stork brought them. When they're a little older, you tell them about love and affection, and when you think they are old enough to understand the answer to the question, they already have figured it out from an older sibling or friend.

At daycare one day, Alex was pulling books off the shelf looking for a special book to read. Buried in the middle there was a children's book about God and the bible. Alex picks up the book and brings it over to us. He points at his playmate, a little baby about 10 months old and says "BABY" and I respond, "Yes." Then he points at the book and says "GOD," and again I say, "Yes."

"God... Baby.. God ... Baby." Then with the most innocent, angelic voice he asks me,

"Ask God Bring Baby?"

After an awkward silence that seemed like two decades, Miss Jane pipes up. "Sorry Alex. You'll have to ask Mommy that question."

Alex tilts his head back to look at her. He responds "Why ask Mommy about baby?"

"Errrrrrrrrrrrrrrrr... ahem... uuuuuuuuuuhhhhhhhhhh..." Cough, cough.

"Time to go home!"

Whew!!

While I can take solace in the fact that he was two, and wasn't really ready to understand the mechanics of human reproduction, I violated a promise that I had made to myself long ago, to always answer his questions, no matter how difficult they seem to be at the time. Afterwards, I wondered how does one answer that question, without confusing the child even more.

~@~

Diary of Missing Keys

Ever have one of those days? You know the one—where one seemingly innocent mistake turns into a series of increasingly complicated missteps that take an eternity to correct? This was the day that if I was smart enough—which obviously I wasn't or I wouldn't be writing this now would I?—I would have crawled under the covers and started the day over - say the NEXT day—when it would be a much better day.

The day started badly. I overslept the alarm and was frantically running around in the morning trying to get ready for the office. Nothing was where I thought it should be—the gremlins had gotten hold of all my essentials and scattered them to the far corners of the house. Cursing, muttering under my breath, I thought I had gotten everything and ran for the bus. I turned the corner to the bus stop as the billow of dust receded in the distance. Plan B: I sprinted to the fallback bus stop - and again missed that bus by a few hundred feet. Huffing and puffing, I jogged to the metro station a good 10 minutes away.

Still, something was nagging me,—something I couldn't quite put my finger on. The rest of the day I had ample warnings and deep thoughts of the impending crisis - but I waived them off, oblivious to their impact. The feeling of impending doom stayed with me till the end of the day. Finally, as I got ready to leave, the feeling again hit me like a sledgehammer in the gut and I realized what I had forgotten: MY KEYS.

I checked my wallet for my spare key. The spare key was missing. Frightfully, I realized that both my primary key and my secondary key were MISSING—and I had to pick up Alex from daycare in about an hour. I called daycare letting them know my dilemma and begged forgiveness for them staying late.

Panicked, I called Candice. Halfway through dialing her number, I realized that she was out of town on a film shoot and there was no way to get in contact with her. Sweat poured off my head as I thought of a solution to my problem.

I asked my co-workers - no one lives close. I asked other friends who work in DC -nada. So I started to make the trek home myself hoping that another opportunity would present itself.

    I arrived at my home station in just enough time to see the community shuttle pull away, again leaving me in the dust, forcing me to walk briskly home. 15 minutes later I arrived at the door—with no key, no plan, and only a faint glimmer of hope. I remembered a spare key I had hidden—but that it was inaccessible since the garage door battery had burned out, and I hadn't quite gotten around to replacing it. I needed a ladder—but from who? I started knocking on doors. No answer. Finally, about half way down the block, I found someone home, borrowed the ladder, and attempted to scale over the fence. The neighbor steadied it as I straddled over, falling and twisting my leg in the process. Hobbling in pain, I retrieved the spare key and entered the house. The neighbor took his ladder and went back home.

    It took me another ten minutes to find the car keys -which were ingeniously wedged deep inside the sofa cushions along with some moldy cheese crackers. I looked at the clock on the wall. I was already ten minutes past final pick-up time

    Now I have the keys, but no car, which is still parked, mockingly, at the other metro station. I will have to ride my bike to get Alex. I took my bike off the hooks in the garage, only to realize that the tires are flat.

    FLAT TIRES?!?!?!?

    "Are ALL the gods against me today?" I cursed in despair.

Back into the house I went to grab the bike pump, throwing on a pair of shorts and an old ratty t-shirt to fix the tire so I could ride to get Alex. Just as I was pulling out of the garage on the now-pumped up bike, another neighbor came home from work--the first good luck I have had all day—and I begged him to drive me to pick up the car. Traffic was backed up on Rockville Pike due to an earlier accident, and we got to the parking garage only to find a heavy metal gate down—the garage had closed 5 minutes earlier.

5 minutes?!?!?!

I ran around back while my neighbor waited and found a small gap under the gate, climbed underneath and descended the 3 levels to the waiting, solitary car.

At long last, I got the car, exited the lot with the automatic keycard waving thank you to the neighbor and arrived at daycare – 45 minutes late. Mercifully, she took one look at me in my disheveledness and did not charge me the late fee I was expecting as a fitting end to my day. In spite of all the obstacles I had overcome to get to daycare, I felt like a complete failure. There stood Alex at the top of the steps, tears streaming down his reddened cheeks thinking that I had forgotten him. Heartbroken, I picked him up and held him, promising to never let him go again.

~@~

Playground Antics

It was a warm spring day. The sun shone brightly through the trees as I ascended the steps to the daycare. Locked? Why is the front door locked? I wondered until I remembered that on sunny days like this the daycare relocates outside and that we go around back to the common area.

As I turned the corner, I heard the unmistakable squeals of laughter you hear on the playground. Alex saw me and ran towards me nearly knocking me over with excitement.

"Come Inside, Come Inside," he implored—tugging at my arm and wanting to show me a toy he was playing with earlier.

"No. No. We're outside now. Let's stay out here in the fresh air."

Again he grabbed my arm imploring me to see the toy. I stopped to talk to Miss Jane to ask her how the day went. Alex released his grip and ran through the open door and into the playroom. He was hunting around for something. After a moment or two, he found it. I saw the gleam in his eye.

Miss Jane saw it at the same time I did. We both bolted for the open door, in what felt like slow motion—arriving moments before he closed the door shut. I jammed my foot in and forced the door back open, in the process knocking the object out of Alex's hands.

The gleam in Alex's eye was because he spied the large block of wood --"My ADT" as it is called - and proceeded to attempt to close and barricade the door. As soon as we were inside, he stepped away.

"Come inside," he said, smiling angelically.

~@~

What does the sheet say?

Every day I pick up Alex from school, and in the general course of collecting his things, I try to engage him in conversation about what he did that day using the sheet that the teacher prepares daily. Sometimes I hear about music class, others about learning a new Chinese word, or others about building some kind of contraption out of Legos. There was one time that Alex said a word in Chinese that both Candice and I greeted him with blank stares. He put his hands on his hips in disgust, "It's Chinese for 'sticker,' mommy."

Often I scan the sheet to ask him questions about what the teacher said he did, lest I get an "I don't know, "Nothing," or "I went to school" answer. It's a good way to get him to open up about his experiences.

On one day, Alex was a bit grouchy and not willing to talk—I knew it had been a tough day just looking at the scowl and the grimace, without even looking at the daily sheet. I asked him "Did you have a nap today?" He muttered something incomprehensible under his breath.

I asked him again. He answered me: "I SAID 'What does the sheet say?'" I looked at the sheet.

"It says you took a nap today."

"Then I guess I took a nap."

If I had talked back like that to my father, I'm sure I would have gotten smacked by the back of his hand or worse. There were just some things you did not do when I was growing up, and sassing your father to his face was sure to leave his mark somewhere on your body.

~@~

The Walkabout

In every parent's life, there are two things that will absolutely terrify you—one is the very first diaper, no matter how much you've prepared for it, and the other is when you look around and the child who is supposed to be a few feet away is nowhere to be found.

Your heart races, your fingertips sweat, as you frantically search for your child—and you now understand why you see parents with proximity alarms attached to their youngsters. All it takes is an unexpected distraction to give them the seconds they need to disappear.

It was the Friday before Mother's Day weekend and Alex's preschool class at his new school had prepared a Mother's Day celebration for all the mothers. However, Candice could not attend as she was on location at a large-scale film shoot out of town so I graciously took her place—and showed up announcing to the odd stares of the other mothers, "The role of Mom will be played by Dad today." I arranged to work from home so that I could attend this event for Alex, though I could not stay because I had several projects to complete.

The children sang their song and we enjoyed our punch and cookies. One by one, the parents packed up to leave with their kids, and as heartbroken as I was about leaving him there till normal pickup time, I said my goodbyes and made my way to the door. Alex clinged to my leg not wanting me to leave. I knelt down, explained one more time to him that I had to go, led him back to the other children playing and, turned once more for the door.

I was distracted for but a moment by another parent asking me a question—and when I looked up, Alex was nowhere to be found. I checked the cubbies... no Alex; I checked the bathroom... no Alex. I checked the puzzle area... no Alex. Looking around, I saw the classroom door had been propped open, so I went down the hall to the fish tank... no Alex. The fear inside me began to build, as I searched frantically up and down the halls... no Alex. I returned to the classroom in a panicked state and marched up to the teachers, interrupting their conversation and said the words all parents dread, "Alex is NOT in the building." And we began to search.

They called the front desk... no one there had seen him. Other staff members joined in, trying to locate him. Time moved in slow motion as we hunted. After the longest five minutes of my life, the classroom phone rang—and at the other end, the front desk person spoke, "we found him" much to the relief of all of us—

especially me. I ran to the front desk and hugged him tightly.

Somehow--and we're not exactly sure how he managed it--Alex had gotten outside the classroom, walked down the hall, surfed out one set of doors behind a departing parent, pushed open the heavy exterior door and walked outside. He made it all the way to the other end of the parking lot before thinking better of it and turning around. The office staff found him outside, banging on the doors to be let back in.

I asked him why he ran away. Alex just shrugged his shoulders and said, "I just wanted to go home with you."

~@~

I was so mad at him that day, he'd already tried to escape – and succeeded – once, that I ended up bringing him home with me after the Mother's Day event. My work projects would have to wait till later, as my home responsibilities now took precedence. We walked in the door and I fixed him a light snack of crackers and grapes. Alex asked for ice cream instead—and after the misbehavior an hour earlier at school, I was not about to grant him his ice cream request. I explained to him, that ice cream is for special treats, and that we weren't going to have ice cream today. Grudgingly, he accepted – or at least he gave me the appearance of acceptance by nodding his head and resuming eating his grapes. Little did I know, that it was actually just a cover story—that he was already plotting his next escape.

When I left the room to change my shirt, he was sitting at the table. I was out of eyesight for maybe two minutes and came back down the stairs. I looked at the table—no Alex. I looked in the kitchen—no Alex. I looked in the bathroom, the alcove and by the toy box - no Alex. I raced up the stairs thinking that he followed me up to the second floor. Nope. Not there either. I raced back downstairs. As I reached the kitchen, I noticed the back door ajar. Out onto the patio I went calling Alex's name. The garage door was up. Now I know I closed it before when we came in the house—so I went to investigate, calling his name with even more insistence. "ALEXXXXXXX." No Alex.

I went outside and started screaming his name—and about a minute later, someone else a block away answered "HE'S OVER HERE." I sprinted down the alley toward the neighbor's voice and found Alex, with his stroller beside him playing with some of the local kids. When I got there, I scooped him up. "Why did you run away from me like that????"

"I wanted ice cream." was the only sound I heard as I put him under one arm, the stroller under the other and marched him back home, his legs futilely flailing in mid-air. Since this was his second dramatic escape of the day, I wasn't taking any chances that there would be a third Houdini-esque grand act, and vowed to keep him by my side until his eyes closed in his own bed that night—with GPS and tracking beacons, if necessary.

~@~

10. Fun in the Sun or a Pain in the Breech

Vacations. Sometimes the only thing we look forward to at work is a long vacation. A chance to unwind, to recharge your batteries, to think and collect your thoughts.

Oh, wait, you brought your young kids with you? Well, you can rule out that relaxing and unwinding part. More likely than not, by the time you are back from your vacation, you'll need a vacation from the vacation. New places to see, new ways to get themselves in trouble, and lots of new distractions to send them off in a wild tangent while you are admiring the local scenery. Don't get me wrong: we've had plenty of fun times vacationing as a family—I just know from my own experiences, vacationing with toddlers is not for the faint of heart.

Our family has always enjoyed cruising. We have been all over the Caribbean, Mexico, Canada, and even a fateful voyage in the Mediterranean accompanied by hurricane force winds. I like it because it is economical, you get a good sampling of vacation itineraries, with fabulous food, exceptional service, and Vegas-quality shows. Plus, it forces me to unplug from my constantly ringing blackberry—which Candice has threatened repeatedly on our trips- that any electronic devices found on my person will fall overboard, never to be seen again. I'm certainly not about to test whether she's kidding.

Alex's first cruise was when he was 11 months old. I predict that one day he will surpass my Grandmother who just completed her 25th cruise, and at 91, is still out partying with the officer staff long after us 'old fogies' have retired for the evening. On that cruise, he occupied his time crawling up and down the staircases. Since then, he's progressed to running the ship like a cruise director-in-training. Ever the ham, people still talk to this day about the two-year-old dressed up in a pillow case toga complete with a golden medallion around his

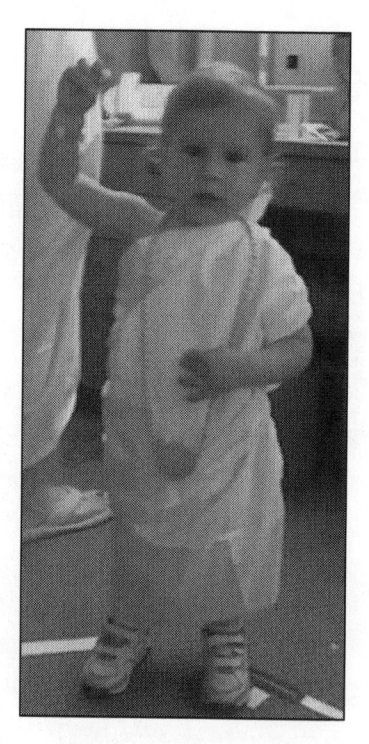

Hail the Toddling Caesar

neck running around the theater, up and down the aisles getting patrons to cheer as the warm up act before the main show.

It seemed that by the end of each cruise, every single passenger over the age of 70 knew Alex—either by name or reputation. There were swarms of former bobby-soxers swooning at his every wink, smirk, and gesture. Everywhere he went, we heard the whispers of his delighted fans—("There's Alex... he's sooo cute... There's Alex, he looks just like my own Alex... There's Alex, he's got such a gorgeous head of red hair on him") And Alex, playing every bit the part, walks into each room waving, and blowing kisses while beaming a brilliant semi-toothless smile.

~@~

Shake your Maracas

It was a sultry but breezy day in Cozumel, and Candice, Alex and I stopped in *Viva! Mexico!*, a local tiki-style bar overlooking the turquoise waters lapping the shore, to get some mango margaritas (for us), and a smoothie (for Alex). As we got to the top of the stairs to the dining room, we noticed that there were several bachelorettes/ sorority girls whooping it up, encouraged by a short, squat, fun-loving waiter known as Rambo. The music was loud, the girls were dancing, and Alex barely two weeks into walking, grabbed his maracas and took a few tentative steps onto the dance floor.

The girls requested "*Shake, Shake, Shake (Shake your Booty)*" from the DJ and as if on command, Alex stood there putting on a show shaking his maracas. One of the girls scooped him up and started to dance with him. Pretty soon all of her friends - the blonde-ettes - were all dancing with Alex. He was laughing, giggling, throwing his hands up and having a grand old time. As I stood on the edge of the dance floor, I wondered if it was possible to be jealous of your one- year-old son - because as sure as I'm writing this - I never had THAT kind of luck with women when I was growing up.

I have a feeling that the event was memorable for him as well—because to this day, every time you hand him the maracas, he says "Shake- Shake-Shake" and does a little dance with a sly, knowing smile.

~@~

I'll Have the Fish, with a Side Order of Indigestion

Dinner meals on cruise ships were not designed for toddlers. They can be two hours or more in length as each course is served. From bread, to soup, to salad, to main entrée, and dessert, it's a moving smorgasbord of gastronomical delight.

...or in our case, gastronomical indigestion.

Each night we'd troop valiantly into the dining room, mirthlessly taking bets on how long we'd last this evening. We prepared a phalanx of surprises... books, cars, toys, pictures, etc. but none of them would hold his attention long. Usually, we had exhausted our bag of tricks far before the third course. The one thing that held his attention was the yearning to explore. It became a game to him: "How can I outmaneuver both Mom and Dad."

So we created a chair barricade to box him in— which only lasted for a moment or two before he circumvented our obstacles and made a break for the door. At first, my reaction was... 'It's a ship - how far could he go?' and took another bite of salmon. As I heard myself think that thought, another, more urgent thought barged into my mind: *It's not the door the dining room I'm worried about - it's the door to the outside deck adjacent to the door of the dining room that could get him into trouble.*

I looked up - he's quietly gotten around the chairs and moved just out of arms reach. As soon as he realized he was free, he made his prison-break escape - sprinting for the open door. Mid-bite, I lunged for the fleeing child- tripping over chairs and trays of food. My toe caught the table leg and I tumbled, doing a face-plant on the carpet, the remains of my salmon dinner slowly oozing out of the corner of my mouth. I watched, arms outstretched, helpless, as my son ran for freedom. Luckily for me, a waiter - who coincidentally played soccer goalie in his hometown before joining the crew— leapt into the path and intercepted the "ball" trying to squirt through the goalposts before promptly returning him to my prone form.

Alex reached over, patted me on the head and said "Hi Daddy." I had become the fall guy to his straight man, so I just lay there and groaned.

~@~

The Next Contestant is... Alex the Cruise Entertainer

By our third day on Costa's *Mediteranea*, a ship decorated like an Italian palace, full of Venetian glass, Tuscan marble, and polished granite, we had gotten the routine down pat. Wake up. Eat. Chase Alex around the boat. Eat. Go ashore. Eat. Come back on board. Eat. The only thing that kept us from weighing as much as the ship by the end of the week was keeping up with the bouncing pinball of a nearly two-year-old. We chased Alex through nearly every public space (and probably a few spaces that weren't). He developed a fascination with the Italian crew members, copying their actions and greetings. He even picked up a few Italian words, (not all of which are printable). All throughout the boat, he walked down the halls saying 'CIAO! CIAO! CIAO!' (A word that means both hello, and good bye). Later, one of the cocktail waitresses taught him 'Ciao! Momma!' and blowing kisses; the transformation to toddling Don Juan was complete. He spent the remainder of the trip saying 'Ciao! Momma!' to every woman he met.

Each night, there was a show after dinner, so we allowed Alex the special treat of staying up to watch - hoping that he'd sleep in the late the next morning. Instead, he'd be the first one up, reaching out of the crib at the first rays of sunlight and saying, "Tickle, Tickle " as he grabbed the soles of our feet and tried to rouse his still-slumbering parents.

The third night's entertainment was the Nunziata twins - Will and Anthony from New York City -- singing a medley of Italian, and New York- Italian songs. During one set, they called upon the audience for participation—they needed some "instruments" for their Italian orchestra. As they asked for a few kids in the audience, Alex leaps off my lap and runs down the aisle. I jumped up to get him – but it was already too late—the entertainers had spotted this not-quite-two-year old running down the aisle and wanted him on their stage.

I turned to Candice, who shrugged her shoulders and said "Why not?" So I scooped him up and carried him down the stairs to where the spotlight shone brightly.

The crowd was abuzz when they saw the toddler arrive on stage. The entertainers busied themselves exchanging pleasantries with their "instruments" what their names were, where they were from, were they an alto or a soprano instrument, etc.

...And then they got to Alex. They bent down and asked him his name. Alex replied quite forcefully, "ALEX," and the crowd went wild. Next they asked him where he was from and he looked at them with a big question mark over his head – so I whispered in his ear "DC" and he repeated "DC"—and again the crowd went wild.

Next, they assigned the instruments to each of the participants—and designated Alex as an Italian Trombone—making the sound "fooooma fooooooma." As they went down the row, each one of the "instruments" made their sounds. They got to Alex as the crowd grew to a hush, and they bent down and asked him to do his sound—and at the top of his lungs he calls out, "FOOOMA!"

The blue-haired ladies in the front row leapt from their seats, clapping so furiously that they nearly went into cardiac arrest.

As the song ended, Alex had one final gift for the audience. Unprompted, he reached over and grabbed the microphone from the performer, blew a kiss to the audience and said "CIAO!"

The entire ship rocked and shook with a thunderous roar.

I stood there on stage behind Alex as my son beamed ear to ear receiving the tumultuous applause, silently basking in my son's charisma, and ruefully cursing myself that this was the night I had left the video camera in the cabin.

Alex with the cruise ship entertainers Will and Anthony

~@~

Boat Music

It was a day at the races—a polo match between US and Italy to be precise. Normally you wouldn't find me in a place like this – too stuffy, too much protocol – and waaaay too much high fashion for my tastes—but it was Mother's Day weekend and Candice had to produce her annual TV show, so we got dressed up and went off to the match. We were the entourage--which was appropriate-- given that the event was attended by multiple dignitaries, movie stars and hosted by a couple who would later become infamous for crashing a White House State Dinner.

I felt like I was in the scene from *Pretty Woman*.

The field was a muddy soup – it had rained heavily the night before and everything was a mess. It was difficult, if not impossible to push the stroller through the muck – so I abandoned it – and for most of the day Alex rode on my shoulders.

As we wandered down the hill we passed the entertainment pavilion. The Italian singers were warming up and singing some of the songs from their show that night. From up on my shoulders, Alex calls out, "BOAT MUSIC."

"Boat Music?" I wondered, "What the heck is Boat Music?"

He pointed at the stage—"BOAT MUSIC."

I pondered it for a few minutes as we stood there listening, as the singers finished their set.

Alex clapped wildly and calls out, "MORE BOAT MUSIC" ... then looking around added "....PLEEEEEASE?!"

And then, like I'd been run over by one of the Polo ponies – it hit me:

The song they were singing was Andre Boccelli's song, "*The Prayer*" – that he had heard on the Cruise ship four months before.

He had remembered the music from our last night on the boat.

~@~

Baby Jane

You never forget your first love—but what do you do when your first love is a showgirl?

To a child, (and to many adults as well) show girls are glamorous and beautiful, with costumes made of exotic feathers and sparkle and beads to turn many a head. Their eyes twinkle in the dusk-light of the stage, flashing like diamonds behind the heavy pancake makeup. Their smiles draw us in, bringing a color to our cheeks and engage a faster beating heart, causing many an audience member to be smitten and forget their dreary lives for but a few moments.

And so it was with Alex.

From the moment he saw her on the gangway, he wanted to meet his golden-feathered goddess. Even when he donned his birthday crown- a cake-shaped hat with three birthday candles and became king of the boat, he ran off in search of his Cleopatra. At dinner every night, he would look for her as she strolled around the dining room, eagerly waiting for the dancing girls in their costumes to make their entrance.

On his birthday night, his wish came true. She was his not-so-secret birthday wish, standing in full resplendent regalia just feet from the dining table and he rushed to meet her. Like many men meeting their vision of love for the first time, he was smitten and tongue-tied, barely able to utter the words "hi." She stooped down and kissed him, her long eyelashes gently caressing his cheek and sending his heart aflutter.

He ran away, telling everyone at the tables, "She kissed me, she kissed me." If it were possible, he would have been running on air as he shared his tale.

The weeks have now passed, and the cruise fading into distant fuzzy pictures, and while life goes on for the three-year-old, any time you mention the cruise, his only memory is that of the girl with the diamond-brilliant smile who kissed him and made his birthday wish come true.

~@~

Turning the Tables

Have you ever been prank-called by a radio station? I can now say that it has happened to me twice in my life. The first, I was a teenager and they wanted to know who was buried in Grant's Tomb or something obscure like that, the second was on the cruise ship, as the entertainment staff had a morning call-in show, and when they needed filler material, would randomly place prank calls to the staterooms.

We were getting dressed for the pool when our phone rang. The English voice on the other end asked the question, "We have an order for 600 cookies, where would you like them delivered?" Having heard this voice several times already during daily announcements, I knew who it was and decided to play along. "We're having a big party down here in our stateroom. Bring them on down and don't forget the gallons of milk from the buffet," we played back to them. After turning on the TV set and seeing that we were live on air as they waved to us, they got us to say where we were from and how much we loved our FunShip Cruise, they hung up and started dialing their next unsuspecting victim, err... passenger.

I placed the receiver down and turned around to a serious stare and scowl from Alex. "WHERE'S MY COOKIES," he demanded. Rather than make up some elaborate lie, or direct him to the buffet, I told him the man on the phone has your cookies. You have to call him to get them." Alex walks over and picks up the receiver. "CALL." He insisted. So I dialed the phone.

On the TV screen behind us I hear the phone ring, and the host answered it. Alex, playing the perfect foil in this caper, takes the phone and asks, "WHERE"S MY COOKIES?!!??!" The host, not quite expecting this interrogation, stumbled and stammered through a semi-quick witted answer.

Negotiator-Alex kept hammering on the host ('I want my cookies...') until the English gentleman agreed to provide cookies. (Where he was going to come up with 600 cookies wasn't even really an issue—it was getting the one for Alex was the problem. The host invited Alex to the show that night, and he would get a special treat. Alex agreed. The deal was struck and we watched on the TV as the host breathed a visible sigh of relief as he hung up the phone.

That night we arrived at the show a little early as we had been instructed. The host saw Alex and welcomed him on stage. As he climbed the steps, he looked over and saw a vision of white—his fantasy girlfriend, the dancer Baby Jane, smiling at him from just off the stage. In her hands she held two presents – one, a plate full of cookies, and the other a ship's trophy (affectionately called a "ship on a stick" by the crew). Alex ignored the host and walked over to his fantasy girlfriend wearing a smile that could have swallowed the Titanic.

Unbeknownst to Alex, Baby Jane, sans glittery costume and stage makeup, had been the co-host of the morning program and remembered him from his birthday candle hat two nights before. She bent down and gave him the specially-made plate with 3 cookies—one for each of the birthday candles.

~@~

Soooo, No Cruise Then?

Every year, usually around Alex's birthday (by coincidence, not necessarily by design—though when you price out kids birthday parties, it makes more sense to go on a week vacation for less than amount you'd pay to host a bowling party with 15 of his closest friends) we take a family vacation. Normally, we take a cruise in the Caribbean, but having visited most of the ports more than once, we expanded our horizons to the Mexican Rivera on West Coast of Mexico.

As luck would have it, the ship was due to depart from Los Angeles a couple of days after Alex's birthday—so as a special surprise, we added a day in Disneyland to the trip. When we made the flight reservations, we realized that we would be landing in Los

Angeles on his actual birthday – so we made plans to go to the Magic Kingdom directly from the airport.

After we landed in the Long Beach Airport, we immediately took a taxi over to Disneyland. As we approached the gates of the House of Mouse, we told Alex that this was his birthday surprise—that we were going to see Mickey for his birthday.

Alex sat there stone-faced. Most kids would be jumping for joy, bursting out of their seats with excitement. Alex showed no emotion. Both Mom and I tried to encourage him—that this was going to be fun that you're going to have a blast. You could tell that he was puzzling over something.

Finally Alex looked up and spoke in a determined monotone: "Soooooooooo. No cruise then?"

~@~

Candy Charmer:

Charm and persistence pays off. I've noticed that when Alex really wants something, he turns on the personality until he gets what he wants.

On day two of the cruise, we were wandering down one of the corridors on the main deck when Alex found the candy shop. Yanking us into the store, he begged us for a bag of candy. Mean parents that we are, refused to give it to him, indicating that dinner was in an hour and that a bag of candy would spoil his appetite. The candy-counter girl smiled sadly and waved as we quickly ushered him out of the store, his arms outstretched in a vain attempt to grab some pieces off the counter, in search of a fountain or something to distract him from his candy quest.

Later that night when we went to dinner, Alex looked up and noticed before we did that the candy counter girl was also the assistant maitre'd. She smiled at him as he marched up to the front desk, "Do you have any candy?" flashing a smile that filled his entire face and lit up his eyes.

Shaking her head sadly, the hostess said "Sorry, no candy," and typed into her computer to assign us to a table.

"I like gummies," he said over his shoulder as we walked into the dining room.

Every night for the remainder of the cruise, Alex would see her at the check in stand, and every night, he would ask her for a bag of candy. Every night he reminded her, he liked gummies.

The final night, he marched up to the stand again. This time the hostess's eyes twinkled as she motioned him to her side. Behind her back, she held a surprise: a bag of gummy worms, gummy bears and gummy fish. Not knowing *WHICH* gummies, she selected a few of each and put them aside for him in a small plastic candy bag. Alex jumped for joy when he saw the bag, carrying it like a trophy to the table like a band major, knowing that he had won out with persistence and charm. He may not have gotten his reward on the first night, but he knew that eventually, if he asked over, and over, and over again, that he would emerge victorious.

~@~

The Safe Cracker

When using an ATM or opening a combination lock, you should always be aware of your surroundings—taking special note of who might be watching you type in your combination. I had no idea that the vigilance also should extend to pairs of eyes at waist level.

Every cruise ship stateroom has a small safe that occupants can place their valuables, passports and jewelry. Given how easy it is for items to get lost in a room the size of a walk-in closet, I tossed the items in and activated the lock. Less than two feet away, a small pair of eyes appeared to be watching cartoons. However, as soon as I went into the bathroom area, the pint-sized safe cracker stealthily approached his target.

The room was silent, except for his footsteps. Too quiet. I heard a cabinet door opening, followed by a mechanical sound, "Beeep. Beeep. Beeeep ... Beeeeeeeep …. *Click*"

Poking my head out of the bathroom door, I noticed two little hands in the safe. He was not taking the contents out—but rather putting them back in. He had memorized the numbers on the keypad, opened the mini-vault door—and was in the process of replacing the contents - (AND CHANGING THE COMBINATION)— when I caught him red-handed.

I predict that I will be keeping a tight rein on my wallet as Alex gets older.

~@~

11. Baby Banter

    From my earliest memories, I remember sitting in my bed as my mother read to me. It was a nightly ritual that we continued for many years. Often, my brother, sister, and I would climb around mom on my bed as she would read to us. Later, as I got older, I read books to them as well—and that has served to foster my love of reading to this day. By kindergarten, I was reading full books to the class, and heaven help me if I wander into a museum where I want to read every placard, signpost and caption much to the chagrin of Candice who would rather see the bullet pointed version. I'd probably still be in the British Museum if a couple uniformed guards hadn't ushered me out the door at closing time.

    I was determined to pass that love of reading on to Alex. Every night for bedtime I try to read him at least one story—and that dedication to words has paid off. Around three months of age, I heard him mimicking words back to me. 'Thank you' became "Ank oo," 'Hi' became "I." I tried "supercalifragilisticexpialidocious" but he greeted me with a blank stare, so perhaps I pushed it a bit too much. I'll just credit Dr. Seuss for Alex's rapid advancement. As I mentioned earlier in the book, Alex's first words were a complete sentence, so it should surprise no one some of amazing things that came out of his mouth. It was the start of what I affectionately refer to as 'Baby Banter.'

~@~

How Are You?

It's always wonderful when your baby does something that surprises you—whether it's a word or a gesture or a phrase that just leaves you speechless. It's even more memorable when they do it in front of an audience—because, as every parent knows, you have WITNESSES who can testify that yes your child did just what you said they did—and not say you made it up. (Most people secretly disbelieve what you say about your own kids, because, well ... you're biased.)

During our trip to the Caribbean on a cruise ship in January, just shy of Alex's first birthday, the three of us were dressed up for dinner. It was formal night, and the men were in their tuxedos, the women in their best ball gowns. Alex was dressed in a stylish jacket and khakis his Grandy (Candice's mother) had given him for Christmas. Everyone was exchanging pleasantries—how good they looked, how marvelous the trip has been, the ship, the staff, etc. Alex, not wanting to be left out, decided to chime in as well.

As we rode up one of the glass elevators, Alex turned to the woman next to us, a mid-sixtyish, silver-haired grandmother decked out in glitter and pearls, and said "How are you?" clear enough that she not only heard what he said, but that she responded to him as well. "I'm fine young man, how are you?" Alex beamed and flashed his trademark grin.

I turned to the other riders and desperate for the validation, said, "I have eight witnesses that he said that. Right? Right? Right?"

~@~

The Thinker

Alex is always pondering. You can see it in his brow as he scrunches it up like the famous Rodin sculpture— *The Thinker*. He often looks like he is just waiting for the right words to say. For instance, Candice has grown frustrated trying to get him to say "Mama" since almost the moment he was born—or at least since he could open his mouth. Every time she feeds him, she'll say, "Say Ma-Ma. MAAAA MAAAAAA. MA MA. You can do it. Maaaa Maaaaa." Alex, stubborn as he can be, does not perform on command. Very rarely does he say it. 'Dad, Dada, daddy'—no problem. But 'Mama' is a completely different story. And when Alex, intentionally or not, responds to her pleas of 'Mama' with 'DaDa,' she calls out to the air, "He's calling for you. Your turn to feed him."

One day Candice made brownies. As they were cooling, the smell wafted into the next room, drawing Alex toddling into the kitchen. He stood next to the countertop pointing at the pan. Candice looked back at him and told him, "They're not for you, they're for my co-workers birthday," which of course, means absolutely nothing to the toddler. It only means that he isn't getting them. Alex continued to point.

Realizing that he wasn't going to get a brownie, he arched his eyebrows, made puppy dog eyes at Candice, cocked his head slightly and said, "MAMA."

Guess who got the brownie after all...

~@~

The crash that you hear is the first thing that gets a parent's attention. Little hands just able to reach the countertops inevitably come in contact with things they shouldn't – and the offending object goes flying. We learned very quickly, that if you didn't want something broken, you put it away. If you wanted something you didn't mind flying, you replaced it with plastic. In spite of our best efforts, things still managed to get broken. You feel yourself getting angry about it, but a deep breath or two later, you have composed yourself so that you don't say something to your child that you will instantaneously and permanently regret.

The second they hear the crash, and see the look in your eyes, they know they are in trouble. Some children flinch and cower. Others burst into tears. Alex puts on a goofy face and launches a charm offensive. It is especially difficult to keep a straight face when they are being mischievous and cute about it. And once you've broken a smile—you, and any punishment or cross words you were even remotely contemplating, are toast. Even at a young age, children comprehend this action innately.

One Friday night we were eating dinner, and Alex decided he was done with his juice. He picked it up, held it out and dropped it off the tray. It hit the ground, dislodged the lid and scattered the juice in a three foot blast pattern—all over the floor, the cabinets, the door, and the recently re-painted wall. He looked down out of the high chair at the mess on the floor, looked back at both of us, cocked his head and said: "UH-OOOOOHH!!"

You grumble, knowing that those three short seconds has created an hour's worth of cleanup work, but you know that it is next to impossible to reprimand when your son is acting like a goofball in his highchair to elicit a smile by any means necessary.

~@~

Honeeeeeeey

I mentioned earlier that I've never been much of a cook --my meals generally consist of anything that could be thrown together in one pot—macaroni and cheese, spaghetti, ramen noodles, frozen vegetables – the basics. However, ever since Candice and I switched schedules, I ended up doing most of the cooking.

It is a challenge for me, and generally takes patience and a good deal of concentration – both things in short supply when you have a nearly two-year old running around disassembling the toy bin for the 1100th time that evening.

One night as I was cooking, I had the rice dish, the vegetable dish and was busy preparing the fish sticks and the tartar sauce. Across the room, Alex was eating a piece of cheese. He had finished the cheese and wanted another—so he's shouting at me:

"DADDY, DADDY, DADDY."

So I leaned back over my shoulder with my hands still on the pots and answered him – "What do you want?"

"DADDY, DADDY, DADDY," he chirped.

Again I turned back to Alex and answered, "What do you want?" getting more than a tad exasperated.

"DADDY, DADDY, DADDY," he chirped again.

This time I ignored him and continued preparing the rest of the meal.

He stopped, thought pensively for a few seconds – and at the top of his lungs called out:

"HONEEEEEEEEEEEEY!!!!"

...said with the perfect tone and inflection of my wife who uses that voice when my to-do list has just grown by another checkbox.

I wheeled around, expecting to see my wife having come home early. No wife. Instead, it is my son who's looking back at me, holding out his empty plate, smiling angelically.

"CHEESE ...PLEASE" he says...

The Inadvertent Salty Sailor

What to do when your child starts talking like an inadvertent salty sailor?

Alex and I arrived home from daycare one day and as I was opening the lock, Alex drops the F-bomb on me. I looked at him and wondered which kid he picked up the word from at school. The word hung in the air like a dense fog.

'Maybe I didn't hear that right,' I thought to myself. 'What did he say?'

So he repeated it.

"Uhhhhhhhh.... Where did you learn that?" I panted, suddenly turning both red in the face and pale as a sheet.

He repeated it again.

"We don't say that word in this house."

He repeated it a fourth time; meanwhile, beads of sweat are forming on the back of my neck. It's getting a tad hot and uncomfortable in the room.

As he's saying the word—he walks over to the video stack on the shelf. Upon reaching the shelf, he looks over his shoulder and says the word a fifth time. The expression on his face said it all: 'Look Dad, you're obviously not getting it. THIS is what I want.'

In his hands he proudly holds out a video for me to see—of a lovable misunderstood green monster that lives in a swamp.

"OHHHHHHHHHH" I say, suddenly very relieved. "You pronounce that:

SSSSSSSSSSSHHHHHHHHHHHRRRRRREEE EEEEEEEECCCCCCCCKKKKK. Can you say it with me? ... SSSSSHRRRRRRREEEEEECCCCCKKKK."

And he said the word a sixth time.

"Not that word ... SSSSSSHRRRRRRRRRREEEEEEECCCCCCKKKKKK

Say it with me ..."

By the seventh time he said it, I'm relatively certain that he knew it got a reaction out of me and was now just saying it for effect. My feeble attempts at dissuading him from using the word had the opposite effect and reinforced it.

The next day, I arrived at daycare just in time to hear Alex say it again, and had to explain to his provider that he wasn't really saying what he was really saying. The former Assistant Principal raised her eyebrows at me. She didn't believe my protestations either.

~@~

Turning the Etiquette Tables

Most parents dream of the day that they hand their child a bowl, or a plate, or a cup, and without prodding, are answered by the words, 'Thank You.'

Alex is remarkably better at this interaction than most toddlers. Routinely, he will answer 'Thank You' without encouragement so often that we have progressed to other social interactions, including the response... "You're welcome."

I'm beginning to think I taught him this social interaction a little too well. One night as I was preparing dinner, I handed him a bunch of grapes for a snack. As I turned back to the counter to continue preparing dinner, he pipes up, "Thank you."

Before I had a chance to turn back to him, I hear him exclaim, "uh.... WELCOME????" with his facial featured and upturned hands contorted in an indignant fashion. My son had turned the etiquette tables on me as I stood there, a man chagrined by my own poor-timed response.

~@~

I'll Have a Double Cheeseburger, Onion Rings and a ….

Every once in a while I get to work from home. More often than not it is not a reason of my choosing. Either one of us has the flu, or I'm home with Alex because of a doctor appointment or a fever, etc. Never knowing what tomorrow brings, I take my laptop home so I can still get the work done during Alex's naps, etc.

One day I was typing away on the computer for a project due later that week while Alex slept in his crib. I've learned from experience that nap time is as much a benefit for the parents as it is for the children because it allows both of us to get stuff done—him to sleep and I to do everything else that piled up. He had been asleep for about two hours and I knew that my free time was running short. In the background over the baby monitor, I heard him start to stir, as he rolled over and stretched. The motions and bumps grew louder as I heard him shuffling closer and closer to the night stand at the end of the crib where the monitor was located. I feverishly finished my work knowing that I only had a few minutes remaining of uninterrupted peace—knowing that at any moment I would hear an insistent cry to signal that the nap was at end.

Over the loud speaker, instead of a cry, I heard a bunch of feedback and commotion. Bump! Frequency Squeal! Bump! And then... silence. I perked up my ears. Next, Alex talked into the microphone, thoughtfully asking, "Daddy bring Juice?"

OK, so that's not unusual. He's asked for that before.

He continues, holding the monitor like a big clunky walkie-talkie that my brother and I grew up with, "I want .... Chicken Nuggets... Corn ..." He thought about it some more. "...And Green Beans... and Scooby Doos (a fruit flavored snack that he gets at lunch)"

I didn't realize I was running a fast food restaurant, complete with toddler-in-window. I think I've got a prepackaged bag of dollar store toys around here somewhere that I can include with his happy meal. Do I deliver it crib-side?

~@~

Etiquette Battering Ram

Language is a subtle art form. It is full of nuance and gesture—and much more is said than is spoken or implied. Take for instance, the simple phrase, "Excuse me."

Most people see the phrase as a means of smoothing over social missteps. You say "excuse me" when you bump into someone, or when you make them stop in their tracks, or any number of moments of social interactions. It is often forgotten by the recipient as quickly as it was said – and only really remembered when it, itself is not spoken.

In the hands of a two-year old the phrase isn't a social nicety-- it's a battering ram.

"Excuse- me," has become Alex's favorite new phrase. He walks down the path and says "excuse me" when he goes past someone else—sort of like how someone would say 'Hi' or "hello" to a neighbor. For him, it gets the interaction he wants ('what a polite boy') and gets people to move out of his way, as if by magic.

One night we went as a family to see the movies on the lawn at the community center. There was a space next to a tree that Alex wanted to sit under. Problem was, there was already a person sitting under it. Alex boldly goes up to the person and says, 'EXCUSE ME'—but the person remained seated.

Alex turned to me, as if to plead his case, "I SAID 'excuse me'," he uttered.

I bent down to talk to him.

"The lady is already sitting there. You'll have to sit somewhere else."

Alex looked thoughtfully at me for a moment, turned back to the lady and said, "EXCUSE ME…. PLEASE."

I blanched at his verbal insistence, and thinking quickly, came up with a toy I had hidden in the diaper bag for some future unforeseen event. Thus distracted, I quickly ushered him away as I apologized to the lady. Now was not the time to explain the subtleties of the phrase to a two-year-old. But Alex wasn't done yet. As we migrated to another spot on the lawn, he waved deliberately as he called out, "See ya later."

~@~

The Spelling Code

As a child, we all heard the secret code of parents. When they wanted to communicate without us understanding, they'd resort to spelling the words out. One day, we figured it out on our own. They'd spell out a word and we'd decipher the code. As a precocious kid of about four, I remember proudly confronting my parents, "I C..A..N..S..P..E..L..L," and proceeded to rattle off the word they had just spelled. Of course, like any spymaster whose communications have been compromised, they changed the code. I think that's how Pig-Latin developed.

I try the same tactic with Alex. I spell "bedtime" or "bath time" or "medicine" –actions Alex detests, or at least moderately despises-- to communicate secretly with Candice. I wasn't prepared to have my slightly more than two-year-old son pick up on my spelling and decipher the meaning – figuring I had at least another couple of years before he'd truly understand.

Dinner was over, so I asked Candice if she wanted to take a walk for some ice cream. I've learned the hard way that if I ask it out loud, I then have to contend with an insistent pint-sized ice cream connoisseur who wants a scoop and, me being the soft-sell that I am, hardly needs convincing- -and off to the ice cream parlor we go. So, on days I'm not sure whether I'm alone in this regard, I'll spell it out to her.

My fatal flaw this day was the speed by which I was spelling the words 'ice cream.' When you run the letters together fast enough—you can hear the word. Alex heard enough syllables to figure out what was being said.

Suddenly he looks up, his face lit up with recognition like a 1000 watt bulb, and jumps up out of his chair, excitedly running over to me and tugging at my shirt.

"YES!! WANT ICE CREAM, ICE CREAM, ICE CREAM."

Candice shot me one of those raised eyebrow glances: "Guess you've got your answer now, don't you?"

And just like that, we were off to Maggie Moos for dessert.

~@~

Waking the Dead

Ever since Candice and I were dating, there has always been one goofy, touristy activity we like doing together. We like to listen to ghost stories. Inevitably, we'll be at Colonial Williamsburg, or Alexandria, VA, or New Orleans and stumble upon a ghost tour. I like them for the storytelling—and for the fact that odd things always seem to happen when we're there—a shadow in the room or a cold spot. (Who knows? Maybe the ghosts are real.) Candice likes them - either because she placates me because I like them, or because she likes getting the shiver up her spine when the person talks about the ghostly apparitions walking through walls.

On one dark and humid-misty night on the campus of William and Mary, Alex attended his first ghost tour. We listened intently as the guide talked about the spectral sightings in one of the administration buildings. She was building to the final conclusion, weaving in an air of mystery and suspense. We held our breath, waiting to find out what happened.

Out in the blackness, dimly lit by the campus streetlamps, a small, determined voice from the path below us pierced the silence.

A.. B... C... D... E... F... G...

Amid the laughter, Alex had written his own ending to the spooky story.

~@~

The Storyteller

Alex becomes very animated when he tells a story. He gestures, drawing you in. When he describes pain, you can feel the hurt; when he describes his joy, you can feel the warmth; and when he describes happiness, you wear his smile in on your heart.

Today, we went to the doctors – to get his yearly flu shot. Alex, like most of us, doesn't like going to see the doctor –particularly when he's going to be poked and prodded. Often, I read him stories in the waiting room to keep his mind off the visit like my mother read to me those many times I got allergy shots as a child. I created voices for the various characters that were the opposite of what one would expect: a deep and dark voice for a female character, a high, squeaky voice for a male character, and a wrinkled old man for a baby. Alex would laugh and tell me, "Babies don't talk like that."

Later that night as we sat down to dinner, Alex recounted the story of his visit to the doctor's office to Mom. Here is Alex's version of the story in his own words:

I went to the doctor.

I'm a big boy.

Daddy talked funny.

Daddy said 'Waaaaaaaaaah'

Daddy not make me cry.

I was scared.

I got an ouchie. [flu shot]

I'm a big boy.

I didn't cry.

The man gave me a lollypop.

He's my friend.

I like lollipops.

And donuts.

I ate donuts with Daddy.

Maybe a bit of my gift of words is rubbing off on him?

~@~

Alex's Greatest Hits

Every parent needs to get away every once in a while—even if it is for a day or so. In late December, Candice and I went away for a quick overnight trip to

New York to see some theater -- *Jersey Boys*, the story about the 50's rock group *The Four Seasons*, take in a wonderful meal, and generally do some sightseeing. It was our first trip away without Alex. Like most nervous-nelly parents, I called my parent's house regularly to make sure that Alex was OK. Of course, since he was having a wonderful time being spoiled by his grandparents, he could have cared less if we were next door or a million miles away.

As a memento of our trip we bought the soundtrack and popped it in the car's CD player, listening to the songs over and over again all the way home to Maryland. The day after our return home, we hopped in the car to go to a birthday party and took our CD out and put Alex's Muppets CD back in. Suddenly a firestorm erupted from the back seat.

"No Kermit. I want SHARI BABY."

"Shari Baby? You want Shari Baby?" I said, shooting Candice a confused side-glance.

"Shari Baaaaby …. and Big Girl."

"Big Girl?" I said arching my eyebrows at Candice.

"Big Girl."

So Candice took out his CD and put in ours. The first song began to play.

"I WANT Shari Baby!" Alex demanded from the back seat.

"Allright. Allright. Here's Shari Baby." Candice said, frantically searching the CD cover for the track number of Shari Baby.

While we were searching for it, Alex belts out:

"Sharrrrrry Baby, She-rr-ry Baby can you come out tonight (bum bum bum)" and then proceeded to mash it together with 'Big Girls Don't Cry.'

Alex's final version of this new song sounded something like this:

"Sherry Sherry Ba a aabie."

"Sherry Sherry Baabie. Can you come out tonight."

(ba bum bum bum)

"BIG GIRLS DON'T CRY BIG GIRLS DON'T CRY" (shouted)

"Big Girls Don't Cry. Big Girls Don't Cry"

"Lollipop lollipop oh lolly lolly lollypop *POP*" (with the mouth popping sound)

Of course I tried to get him to sing it again at home—this time for the camera. Upon seeing the camera he turned defiant, refusing to utter a note. Instead of enjoying the moment for what it was – a moment, a private concert meant only for his parents' ears--- I tried to turn it into something more, and lost its magic. It was never meant to be recorded, but only to exist within our own hearts and memories.

Actually Approximately

Sometimes I look at Alex and think he's just a baby. Other times I look at him and wonder how did he get to be so grown up—and then there's those times when he says something so out of character that you wonder if he's really a regular on *Masterpiece Theater*, trapped under a malevolent spell in a pint-sized body.

As we walked home from daycare, I asked him what he wanted for dinner that night—to which he answered Scoobiee Dooooos.

"No," I told him, "You can't have Scoobiee Doooos for dinner. Try again." I asked him a second time, "What do you want for dinner?"

"Nothing," he flippantly replied.

"OK ... then you get nothing, if that's what you want." I replied, giving him no negotiating room.

I've learned from past experience with him that if I give in even the slightest bit, Scoobiee Doooos will most likely end up the before dinner snack and spoil his appetite. We strode on in silence, him defiantly kicking the pebble on the sidewalk and I walking beside him. As we reached the garage door, he turned to me and said: "Actually, I'm approximately very hungry."

I thought about it for a few moments and smiled to myself as I turned the key in the lock. "Actually, that is approximately, a complete and accurate sentence."

~@~

You're not my friend.

Every once in a while, kids will come home from day care adopting a term or phrase that you rather wish they wouldn't—often from hearing another child speak it on the playground. Even when the other child gets reprimanded for it by the teacher, it demonstrates to all of the children that by saying the phrase, you get attention. As any toddler, (Starlet or Public Relations executive) can attest—Attention—whether positive or negative—focuses others' energy on you.

I brought Alex home from school one night and started to make dinner. Several toys were scattered about from the previous night and I asked Alex to pick them up, and was subsequently ignored as Alex focused on turning on the TV set.

"Please put the toys away."

(Silence)

"Alex, I asked you to put your toys away."

(Silence)

"Alex, for the last time, put the toys away, or I'm turning off the TV set until you do."

(Silence)

With that, I walked over to the couch, grabbed the remote and turned off the TV set. THAT got his attention, as he leaped up from the couch, hands clenched as though ready for a fight.

"Turn the TV on."

"No, I asked you to clean up your toys," as I bent down to hand him his first toy. "Please put it away."

Alex threw the toy down in disgust. "YOU"RE NOT MY FRIEND," he yelled, stomping on the floor for effect.

"I'm not your friend, I'm your father. Put the toys in the toy box."

Alex, who clearly wasn't expecting a response thought for a moment and screamed back, "YOU'RE NOT MY FATHER."

"Yes I am," I glowered. "I have the bags under my eyes to prove it."

With nothing left to say to that response, he folded his arms squarely across his chest and stomped deliberately out of the room.

The next night, the battle resumed. The toys were back on the floor, and I refused to let him turn on the TV until they were back in their box. Before I could get a word in, Alex shouts out, "You're not my friend... and ... you're not my father, too."

I just had a foreshadowing of what life is going to be like in ten years when he becomes a teenager.

~@~

Dot-Com It

Not to date myself too much, but when I was a teenager, our family got our first computer – a Toshiba T-100-- similar, yet still inferior to the Apple *IIe* that my much cooler friends had. It was command interface, clunky, and did not do anything except word processing and text-based games. The current generation has grown up with computers all their lives an integral part of their social DNA. I remember I was in college in 1994 when I was first introduced to this new program called Mosaic. (i.e. The first web browser and precursor to Netscape.) We sat around the computer lab marveling that you could point and click a mouse and it actually went to another page--truly revolutionary at the time. Fifteen years later, the technology has advanced so far that you can do much, much more than we ever dreamed possible.

Alex was looking for a TV show he had seen advertised a few days earlier. We scanned the schedule and could not find it listed. I told him, "Sorry, it's not on right now. I guess you'll have to wait until next time it comes on."

Alex looks up from the couch, and matter-of-factly stares me in the eyes—"Daddy," he says in a huff, "just 'Dot-com' it." Sure enough, with Google and a few keystrokes later, we found the episode in its entirety online available for his immediate viewing pleasure.

~@~

12. Not All Fun and Games

I am the first to admit that we are lucky to have a relatively healthy child. There are so many other kids who have chronic illnesses, deformities, or other concerns like autism that make it a challenge to care for them. Yes, he gets colds and the flu from the germ factory known as school almost on a monthly basis, but in general, he has been very healthy, and we are blessed by that good fortune.

... Except when we are not. In any life, you have both ups and downs—and as prepared you are for the ups (what every parent hopes and waits for and drives our decisions to have children) we are often ill-prepared for the downs. All it takes is a few seconds of distraction to change your good fortune.

There's an old expression—never drive faster than your guardian angel can fly. The same applies to babies who try something new when they're not quite ready to do it yet. In this case, it should be, never fall faster than your guardian angel can catch.

Like the mythical Icarus who flew too high too fast and had his wings melted by the sun, Alex reached too far and came crashing to earth, tumbling down the steps. He had been walking for only a few months, when he started growing cocky, bounding up and down the steps with abandon. However, the fates reminded him one night when he was about 16 months old that he still has some learning and growing to do. One moment he's standing on the 2nd step and in the split-second I turned to flip off the light, I look back and he's in a pile at the bottom of the stairs, unable to stand and earning himself his first official trip to the emergency room with a broken leg. I know it's a simple fracture—an easily repaired "toddler fracture" --but it still doesn't assuage my feelings of guilt that I broke our baby by not hovering over him every second.

At what point do you draw the line between over-protection—never letting your child do anything, lest they fall and break a bone, and giving them the freedom to explore to grow up independent and self-assured? I've always been a proponent that kids need to be watched at an arms- length distance – far enough to give them the freedom to try something new, but close enough to step in if they are really in danger. Bumps and bruises are a fact of life. You can't protect them from everything, and really shouldn't even try. Those dents are what help build character and help define us as a person. It only takes a single moment of overconfidence to reach too far and tumble out of the heavens both he and I learned that day. The Greeks call this hubris—I call it humble pie.

Ironically, the cast has not slowed him down. If anything—it's made him crawl quicker. He can get from point-to-point faster crawling than he used to do walking—which only means that when the cast comes off—the drag racer will be back - stronger and speedier than he was before. Until then, he's found other ways to entertain himself.

I came home from a meeting one night to find Alex on the couch in the den. He was sitting up and holding his injured foot in the air. Looking closer, I noticed something odd: He had taken two blue stackable cups and had placed them on the end of his casted foot and proceeded to balance them on the edge of his toes.

He was in the cast for a little more than a month, when the doctor pronounced him fit to resume active walking. After 30 days of lugging a cinderblock around on his right leg, Alex was officially a castaway. It took him, maybe five steps to get his rhythm back, and as soon as he did, he was running farther and faster than he had before the accident. I think I heard the wind whispering, "Run, Alex, Run" behind him as he sprinted. The next day, we went to a pick-your-own- fruit farm at Butler's Orchard as a treat to gather blueberries.

Alex had never tasted blueberries before, and no sooner did he pluck one off the bush, did his taste buds come alive. He demanded more and more of the delicious berries, emptying our bucket nearly as fast as we could fill it. With his hands and mouth covered in purple goo, we ushered him away so that we could finish picking. In spite of his attempts, we filled the buckets, paid for them at the fruit stand, and brought them home.

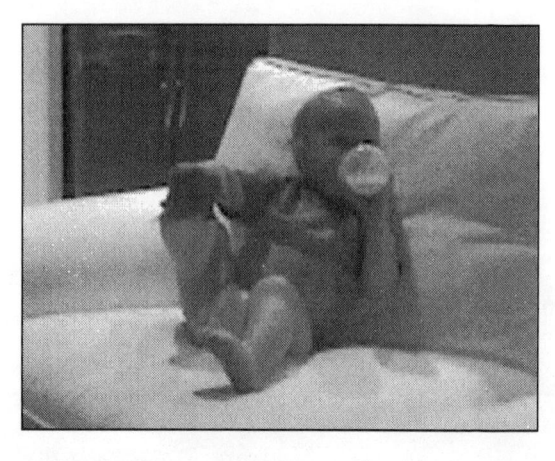

The entire way home, Alex struggled in his car seat to reach over and get the container of blueberries, tantalizingly placed just out of arms length. He grabbed at it, pleading with us for the blueberries. As Alex had already eaten enough blueberries to turn into a blueberry, we told him he was done. Frustrated, he stared longingly at the bucket and plotted his caper.

We arrived home. The phone was ringing-- so we put Alex down on the floor and the bucket of berries on the countertop. In the 15 seconds it took us to answer the phone, he pulled himself up on the couch (something he's never done before) climbed to the top of the couch, and straddled the kitchen island shelf to get at the bucket. He reached over, pulled the bucket closer and proceeded to stuff his mouth full of the sweet treat—blueberry juice oozing out of the corners of his mouth creating a mischievous purple goatee over a wide and beaming smile.

We pulled him down off the island, lest he end up right back in that cast again, only to watch him scamper back up the sofa and start again. By his third attempt, we decided the room defenses had been permanently breached. Candice took "purple boy" to the bathroom to wash up, and I hastily reconfigured the furniture.

If I wasn't present at his birth, I'd swear he's part mountain goat.

~@~

The Longest Train Ride

I was at work at my desk at 2:48PM when the call came in—the call no parent wants to hear. "Hi this is the [Daycare center]. Your son fell in class and cut his head. Medical personnel are on the way. Do we have your permission to put Alex in the ambulance?"

AMBULANCE?!?!?!?!

My heart stopped for a moment. "Yes... Yes you have permission," I stammered. What happened?!?!?

"He fell and hit his head." I started to get the details from the office staff. "He's going to be OK. He just needs a few stitches."

"STICHES?!?!?" I interrupted.

The cell phone in my pocket buzzed. It was Candice. The Daycare center had called and left the message on her voicemail. Knowing how panicked she would be, I answered the cell phone. "[The Daycare's] on the other line there's been an acci-

Candice cut me off. "Alex is hurt. We've got to go to him NOW." She called him Alex, when she normally calls him Sparky. I could tell how panicked she was by that alone and the tone of her voice. I turned back to the other phone on my ear. "We're on our way." I said as I hung up both phones.

Both of us work downtown, and take the metro to the office—which on a good day takes 45 minutes or more to get from one end to the other. I slapped my laptop closed, shouted something to my boss on the way out the door, and sprinted for the train.

Miraculously, the train pulled in as I made it to the platform. A few stations later, I saw a familiar face sprinting down the escalator—barely making it onto the train car ahead of me milliseconds before the doors closed. That, in and of itself is another rarity – on any normal day that we try to coordinate schedules, one or the other of us has to wait 15 minutes or so meet up with the other person. Today it seemed that even the angels were on our side. I changed train cars at the next station and caught up to her. We embraced and sat down on the old and worn leather seats holding each other's hand—the entire trip we barely said a word, lest we give voice to our unspoken fears. A clenched grip, in spite of the white knuckles, offered a few moments of solace and reassurance.

A lot of thoughts run through your head while you sit in silence. That commute which seems excruciatingly long on a regular day becomes interminable as the seconds creep by. You focus on every squeak, creak, and bell to dull the phantom pain – but in your mind there is no reward of peace. You go mad listening to the voices in your head.

We emerged from the darkness as the metro rattled on ascending to daylight and we instinctively checked our cell phones. "No calls—that's a good thing, right?" I asked nervously. Candice nodded silently.

By the time the train reached the platform we had risen from our seats and inched over to the entrance, nearly on top of it as if our squeezing through the aluminum frame would get us to Alex's bedside that much sooner. The doors slid open and we sprinted upstairs, discovering the shuttle bus the angels had delayed. We raced, breathless, and climbed aboard.

Unlocking the house, we sprinted from one side to the other, scooping up the favorite toy and blanket. "He'll need these." I whispered, arms outstretched like a sprinter in a relay race, and ran to the garage. We drove to the hospital barely allowing enough time for the garage door to open.

The angels flew ahead of us, turning the lights green as they went, and finally 52 minutes after we got the call, we burst into the emergency room and were taken to Alex's bedside where a nurse attended him.

On the gurney sat our stoic trooper with an oozing semi-circle gash above his right eye. The angels had turned his head at the last second. A few millimeters either way and he would have gouged his eye out.

In spite of his obvious pain and discomfort, he cracked a wide, half smile, boosting himself up to a sitting position. As we hugged him tighter than we ever had before, he leaned over our shoulders and began reading the letters off the sign above him. A... B... N... Triangle. For the first time since I got the call, I exhaled deeply. In spite of the 14 stitches that turned him into an insta-pirate, just in time for his class pictures the next day, my son was going to be all right.

~@~

In sickness and in health

The month of October was a bad month in the Stankus household. Over the span of four weeks, we visited the emergency room three separate times. The first, for Alex slicing his head open at school, the second for contracting H1N1 (swine flu) and the third about two weeks later with Croup, coupled with complications from the swine flu that earned him a hallway full of paramedic personnel and a second trip in an ambulance. As we entered the now-familiar triage room, I stone-facedly asked Candice if Emergency Rooms have frequent visitor cards.

During the swine flu epidemic, none of us were immune. Alex picked it up from a classmate, I got it from him two days later, and Candice had a much milder reaction. Usually it's the other way around—I get ill for a day and she's down for a full week. I can honestly say it was the sickest I've ever been in my adult life.

If you have ever taken care of a child with the flu, you know what an emotionally draining experience it is. If you have ever tried taking care of a child while you have it too, it's a thousand times more difficult.

All you want to do with a 104 degree fever is crawl up in the fetal position and sleep—a sleep made impossible by the little figure lying next to you, kicking you in the shins every two minutes and shouting "TISSUE!!" in a disembodied nasally voice sounding eerily reminiscent of Golem searching for a ring while pointing a crooked finger at his nose.

After two days that seemed to drag on forever, I finally sensed a break in the storm clouds. Instead of shouting 'Tissue' every few moments, he alternated his 'Tissue' demands with shouts of 'Doritos!' and 'cartoons!'

~@~

13. A Sprinkle of Extraordinary

A couple of years ago I tried an experiment: I asked a handful of random people to relate their fondest memory. Some related meeting their husband or wife for the first time, others told of watching their son or daughter squashing their first birthday cake with their foot, or draw a picture of a scribbled flower and giving it to them. Others told of receiving a favorite present or running the bases at a major league baseball game. To a person, the favorite part that they remembered was not necessarily the event itself—but the remembrance of the extraordinary happenings within the ordinary event.

Life is a series of ordinary events punctuated by the extraordinary—and that extraordinary, is what happens every day if we are observant enough to catch it. I resolved that when Alex was born, I would record as many every day events, punctuated with extraordinary happenings. Alex may not remember any of them now, but someday, when he has children of his own and they ask what he was like as a child, I hope that he can open up this book and smile.

~@~

Alex-zilla

For Alex's first birthday, we got him a wooden train set, some assembly required. Two days before his party, I set out to decipher the hieroglyphics that approximate the step-by-step instructions for assembly. Sometime, some four hours later and well after midnight, I completed the masterpiece—including the metropolis that the train runs through on its journey. I went to bed feeling like I climbed Mt. Everest—or at least that I had just constructed Mt. Everest out of popsicle sticks and Play-Doh.

The next day, we had managed to keep Alex out of the kitchen until nearly bedtime when we had to give him a bath in the sink. He has this huge, forest-green dinosaur towel that we dry him off with after his bath. As we lay him down on the floor to dry him off, he spotted the new toy, rolled over and escaped from our grasp. The naked baby with the green dinosaur towel on his head stood up and lumbered toward the train table. Upon reaching the table, he knocked apart the Golden Gate Bridge, destroyed the airport and set his sights on the port of Los Angeles. With a train in one hand, a piece of track in the other, he looked over his shoulder and started to screech like the monster from the 1950's movies.

If you close your eyes, you might just see the biplanes circling the green creature. And thus, Alexzilla, 'Son of Godzilla,' was born.

~@~

The New Entertainer

Dusk turned to night in Grandy's 17th floor apartment in San Francisco overlooking the Bay Bridge. One by one, the rays of sun were replaced by the neon bulbs of night, and the entertainers come out to play. The lights twinkled off the fixtures in the room, carefully placed, just so, and meticulously maintained. It is not a place that has ever seen small children, and we were cognizant and vigilant with a toddling pinwheel loose among the artwork. Still, even then, Alex managed to turn the kitchen inside out.

At bath time, we decided that we were safer in the kitchen sink than among the perfume bottles and Tiffany Blue boxes that decorated the bathroom. Lacking anything remotely resembling tub toys, Grandy gave him some funnels and measuring spoons. Pretty soon there was more water on the countertop than in the sink as Alex used the funnels to pour water, and Grandy stood there stoically biting her lip as we wiped up the mess.

Sensing Grandy's discomfort, Alex looked at her and got a brilliant idea in his head. Standing up in the sink, he takes two funnels, one in each hand, and places them on his chest, beaming brightly.

At that moment, Candice glances over, sees the funnel placement and asks him – "Are you Madonna?"

Alex arches his back to look up at her from the tub, and began repeating: 'Madonna,' 'Madonna,' 'Madonna', 'Ma-DON-na.' Then, for added dramatic effect, swivels the funnels still cupped to his chest back and forth. Everyone in the room turned to watch, and even Grandy forgot about what a topsy-turvy mess her kitchen had become. We all cheered.

As if he needed more encouragement, Alex, seeing that we were laughing, dropped the funnels and began to clap –making us cheer all the louder.

I saw in him, the lights of the city streaming and glistening. Later that night, as he tried on Grandy's leopard print shoes, I remarked that there is something magical about the City by the Bay that makes entertainers of us all.

White Men Can't Dance

Warning! Two-year-olds cause flashbacks.

There are buried deep within us, awkward memories of our youth, which we have successfully repressed. We never think about them as we have moved beyond it-or have we? Still, having a two-year-old nearby is apt to bring those junior high flashbacks bubbling back to the surface.

Many years ago, I realized I have no coordination, but as stubborn as I was, refused to believe it at the time. I mistakenly believed that *everyone* can be somewhat athletic if they just practice long enough. It took me seeing myself in a video of a middle school basketball game and hearing the coach utter, "Jump, Paul, Jump," every other sentence to come to the realization that a career in the NBA just wasn't even a remote possibility for an uncoordinated white kid from suburban Philadelphia. Today I live with the fact that I am more likely to trip over a sidewalk than to sink the game-winning basket.

Every once in a while I still have those delusions—and every once in a while they come to a screeching halt. Two-year-olds will do that to you.

It was the end of a rather long day – I had just picked up Alex from daycare and brought him home. He was tired. I was tired. I didn't want to just sit on the couch sprouting mushrooms—so I strode over to the satellite receiver and turned on some dance music.

'Come on, let's dance,' I implored— as Alex sat there on the couch and looked at me with this blank stare that said 'just go away.'

But I wasn't going to take no for an answer.

So I went over to him and started to do a wacky dance—a dance that people who think they can dance would do in a mirror.

Again I implored, grabbing his hand, 'Come on let's dance.'

Alex grudgingly hopped off the couch and sauntered over, touching me lightly on the elbow. He looked up into my eyes, shook his head sadly and with a stern/ serious look on his face shattered the fragile remains of my psyche into a zillion little pieces.

"Daddy... No Dance," he said.

...And when even your two-year-old says you can't dance – you know it's time to hang up the clogs.

~@~

The Keurig Barista

For several months, Candice had been eyeing a single-use "pod" coffee maker at Bed, Bath, and Beyond. It gleamed in stainless steel from the shelf of the department store, beckoning her closer. Every time she saw it, I could see droplets of drool gathering in the corner of her mouth. For our anniversary, I let her pick out her favorite one and take it home with her-- a Keurig, that she claims makes the perfect cup of coffee. Not being a coffee drinker myself, I take her word for it.

This coffee maker has a shiny silvery metal handle that is raised and lowered like an old-fashioned soda fountain. You lift the handle up, the previous pod pops out, and you replace it with the new pod. The first week it was home, I think Candice made enough cups to increase the Gross National Product of Costa Rica tenfold.

By Friday, after several days of watching Mom, Alex wanted in on the action. He pushed his chair over to the countertop, and began opening and closing the handle, examining the mechanism to figure out how it worked. Candice showed him where the pods were kept, and suddenly she had a new helper in the kitchen. Every morning he insisted that he should make the coffee. Candice let him load the coffee pod, wait for the fluorescent blue blinking light and press the buttons. It was his new task –and a task he thoroughly enjoyed-- pushing just the right buttons to fill the cup and asking Mom to take it when he was done.

A couple weeks later, we traveled to my sister in-law's, in-laws' gourmet log cabin in the Poconos to share Thanksgiving Dinner. Immediately upon entering the kitchen, Alex spied the coffee maker—the same one he had at home. Scanning the room, he found the stepstool and rushed over to it, tugging it over to the countertop.

"He likes to make coffee," Candice intoned, as she scooped him up and had him fill up the water container and placed the mug under the dispenser. Alex opened the coffee drawer, retrieved the pod, placed it in the opening and closed the silver handle. There he waited—looking plaintively over his shoulder, for the permission to continue. With a slight nod of acknowledgement from Mom, he pressed the blinking blue LED buttons on the coffee maker, and stood back as he had been taught to do, as the brownish liquid began to trickle out and the intense aroma began to fill the air. Soon, the transformed water stopped flowing, and expert barista that he is, knew that he needed a second button push to fill up the large mug.

Candice reached for the cup and sipped it, pronouncing it the best cup she had ever tasted and showered Alex with praise.

Encouraged by the praise, Alex went up to each person in the room and asked them if they would like a cup of coffee. In no time at all, the Keurig barista was whipping up mugs of steaming hot java for all of the house guests. By the time he was done, he had made coffee for 12 different people. I retreated to my long-time ago familiar role as a waiter and dutifully served all of the patrons.

Added to the home-made bread he had baked the night before in our bread maker, Alex had all the ingredients to open his own little coffee shop on that mountaintop by the lake in Pennsylvania—and given how well he brewed the coffee, ensured that his establishment would be humming and well-caffeinated all day long.

~@~

Late Night Computers

Computers fascinate Alex. He enjoys clicking the mouse, opening and closing the CD-ROM drive, putting things in that shouldn't be there and watching me scramble to retrieve them before the drive gets wedged open. He has his own games based on his favorite toddler TV shows that he clicks and manipulates at ease. Often, when it's too cold to go outside, the two of us will sit in the chair, him on my lap and he'll show me how to play his game. It's a sense of pride for him that he can show his dad how the game works.

One night, he told me that he wanted to do it himself—so he banished me to the second chair where I became the onlooker, no longer the participant. I watched as he played the entire game on his own without any help from Dad. At the end of the game, I turned on the printer, printed out his completed game card, exited the program and put the computer into sleep mode before pursuing other projects.

The next morning I was in the computer room, and noticed something odd—the game was back on the screen. I know I had closed it out the night before—but it was back on – and had been obviously played recently. It couldn't have been Candice, who never in a million years would play a computer game—and it definitely wasn't me—so I turned to our not-quite-three-year old computer wizard.

"Did you play the game?" I asked softly.

"I played 'yardigans."

"I can see that. When did you play 'yardigans?"

"I woke up."

"When you woke up you played 'yardigans?"

"Yes. I printed it."

"You printed it?" I asked, turning on the printer.

"I clicked the blue button."

Sure enough, as soon as the printer warmed up, out churned his game piece. A month before his third birthday, he had woken up, wandered upstairs, turned on the computer, played the game that we had only done once or twice together, successfully gotten to the end, and printed it out. The only thing he had not done was turn on the printer. The game piece sat, a pleasant mid-morning surprise for the creator's father. The wheels whirred and chugged, putting ink to paper with a clat-clat-clat that sounded almost like the machine was giving Alex a round of applause. Silently in my mind I was giving him the same uproarious round of applause as well—for this was definitely a job well done.

~@~

The Pool Walkabout

Is it genetic? Do most boys—no matter how old they are—naturally gravitate to girls in bikinis? I think it must've been pre-programmed in our genetic code many, many eons ago—because it just seems that even at a young age, Alex apparently naturally understands that 1) yes, they are women, 2) yes, they are wearing bikinis, and 3) yes, he should walk over to them and try to flirt with them.

It was a sunny Saturday afternoon, and I took Alex to the community pool. While we played in the shallow end, he kept glancing over to the corner of the pool where several 20-something girls were sunbathing, talking, giggling and generally having a good time. We'd splash a bit—and he'd play... but his glances always returned to the beauties at the end of the pool.

Suddenly, he tired of playing in the pool, walked out of the shallow end and made a lumbering beeline towards the girls. I jumped out to block him, but he maneuvered between the chairs and got around me. I attempted to shepherd him back to the kiddie pool but he'd escape, dodge, go back and resume course. After about five minutes of this back and forth, my dripping wet footprints on the deck resembled the dance step cutouts of the rumba or the cha-cha. Tiring of his antics, I gave up and let Alex walk - carefully placing myself between him and the edge of the water. We reached the end of the pool—where the bathing beauties had congregated.

I attempted to guide him past the chairs—but Alex danced just out of reach, giggling and playing peek-a-boo. When I played peek-a-boo back, he wasn't interested—he was focused on the girls behind me. It became unquestionably apparent that I was an afterthought—that his real intention was to get the girls' attention.

The girls looked up from their conversation, eliciting more giggles from Alex. One by one they sat up on their lounge chairs peering over the rims of their darkened sunglasses to see who had invaded their space. All eyes, with the exception of the one pair who trained her dagger gaze on me as if I had put him up to it, were on Alex as he hopped and danced.

~@~

The Stocking Encounter

As a guy, there are many stores that I loathe to go into. Victoria's Secret is one of them. Every time I walk in with Candice I feel that I should be fitted with an Orange Jumpsuit just for being in there, or I'm so busy trying to divert my eyes that I walk into a store display and bump into a skimpily dressed mannequin.

Inevitably, I end up taking a walk through the mall for a few minutes. Secretly I think the store was designed that way to intimidate men—the ones that want to be there are on a mission – ('I want THAT for my girlfriend') and the ones that are dragged in, make a quick excuse to depart, allowing the women to shop in peace.

One night (Every night?) they were having a sale. Nothing draws a woman into the store faster than the word 'SALE!' and leaves us husbands needing to occupy our time. I left her at the store, and Alex and I went upstairs to one of the restaurants, got one of those flashing light-buzzers that tell you when your table is ready and kept feeding quarters into the strategically placed rides just outside the restaurant that have preempted many an impatient toddler's meltdown and spoiling the meal for everyone else. She said 15 minutes. But as any hapless husband waiting outside a lingerie store can attest, 15 minutes is not 15 minutes. 15 minutes is the amount of time she's allocated for browsing. Double that, if it involves actually buying things. At 25 minutes – with the round disk now beeping and buzzing, we went back downstairs. We found Candice in line behind several other women waiting to check out.

"How much longer?" I asked, showing her the buzzer.

She gauged and she figured and calculated in her head. I could see the gears whirling furiously underneath her auburn tresses.

"About five minutes" the answer spit out of her mental sales-calculator computer already whirring and calculating above her torso.

So we waited. I'm trapped in the lingerie store with no place to go. Next to me is an eight foot tall poster of an underwear model whom I'm trying to avoid making eye contact with.

I was so busy trying to not look at the poster, that I wasn't paying as much attention as I should to my little charge. I looked down, and in a fit of panic realized that he had wandered away. Scanning around the store, I found him on the far side near a frilly, lacy display. I looked at him. He looked back at me. "Daddy, it's smooth," he said, running his hand down the mannequin's silk stocking-covered leg. "I'll take this one," he stated matter-of-factly.

I turned flush. Partially angry, partially embarrassed, and partially wondering where in the heck he learned that, I grabbed his arm and yanked him out of the store. "Come on, let's go. This isn't a place for you till you're older." (...or perhaps, even then.)

~@~

Squishy Belly

In October, we found out that our extended family was going to have a new addition—my sister announced that she was pregnant. We explained to Alex that he was going to have a new cousin—that Aunt Janel was going to have baby—and that the baby was growing inside of her.

We tiptoed gingerly around the topic, lest the conversation turn to a different line of questioning I'm not even remotely ready to answer and won't be for nearly another decade. We explained that when he was a baby, he was inside of Mommy's tummy as well.

Alex looked thoughtfully for a moment, perked up his eyes and said, "I remember being in Mommy's tummy. It was warm and squishy inside."

~@~

Romance by the Blue Checkout Light

Shopping at big box warehouse stores can be daunting. Oftentimes, Candice and I divvy up responsibilities – she does the shopping, and I take Alex and go order dinner. As I looked at the long line snaking around the concession stand, I knew that tonight Candice had gotten the better end of the deal.

Behind us in line was a girl of about three in a stroller decked out with ruffles and lace like a princess and her mother, busily talking on the phone and not paying any attention except to nudge the carriage forward a couple of inches. Alex looked at the girl and smiled. She didn't notice him at first. He smiled at her again, this time he added a dance and a wave to his "pay attention to me" routine. She clearly saw him but chose to ignore him.

Alex upped the ante. He walked like a duck towards her cocking his head side to side until their eyes met. Finally she cracked a smile, and taking his cue, Alex saddled up next to her.

He asked her name, and gave his in return. They made goo-goo eyes at each other. He tried to tell her about a book they read in class that day, but it was a book she didn't like. She told him that book is bad—by the way she said it, you could tell Alex was crestfallen. The misunderstanding grew, and Alex grew frustrated, finally leaving her side and coming back to me. Realizing what she had just done, she tried to make amends, but Alex had already moved on.

In the span of those few short minutes and unbeknownst to the oblivious mom still talking on her phone, the two had wooed, had met, had fallen in love, had a spat, a break-up, an attempted reconciliation, and a parting of the ways—a full relationship by the blue light of the checkout stand.

~@~

Money for Thomas, Money for Big Toys

While visiting my parents, Alex discovered the concept of money—that these coins and pieces of paper could be used to exchange for something valuable.

We had gone out to dinner as a family—and out front of the restaurant was one of those coin-operated mechanical toys that we all rode in as kids. Instead of a rocket, this one was of Thomas the Tank Engine. Dutifully, I pulled out my wallet and gave him a couple of quarters to put in the machine. It whirred and sputtered to life, chug-chug-chugging along, the children's songs playing like an old-time Victrola connected to a scratchy, out-of-tune speaker. Alex loved it. A minute later, the ride was over and Alex reached out his hand for more quarters. Resignedly, I gave him my last two quarters and it started up again.

Later at dinner, Alex was playing with his toys at the table while we waited for the food. Suddenly, he lit up with an idea. He hopped out of his chair and marched over to me wanting more quarters for the Thomas ride. Since I was unable to help him out, he went to each person at the table, put his hand out and asked, "Quarter Please," getting enough quarters for several more rides.

The next day we were visiting a relative who owned a fishing boat, and he brought Alex on board, sitting him in the Captain's chair. Alex looked around on the steering column, turned to his Great-Great Uncle and said, "Where do the Quarters go?"

We all laughed knowingly – not because of his innocent question, but because we all knew that it would take more than a few quarters to power the boat – given that maritime gas had just hit $4.00 a gallon and continued to climb.

~@~

Measuring Up

Every year we attempt to do one major house-related project. We try out several ideas and pick the one we need the most, cost the least, or just have to have. One year it was painting rooms, another it was installing shelves, or building a patio, etc.

This year, Candice requested us (and by us, she usually means me) install a granite ledge on the end of the center island. Dutifully, I went to the home improvement store and half-heartedly, got the price quotes, not really wanting to start the project. Deep in my heart I knew that it was beyond my limited ability to install, and determined that I'd need to get a professional in to either do the job – or pay 3x more to fix the job after I started it.

So I dawdled – as any reluctant husband with a "honey-do" list would do.

I hemmed and I hawed, and tried to feign interest—so I did the rough calculations. I pulled out the measuring tape and determined how much material was necessary, adding in an extra 20% or so for the usual cost over-runs.

Finally, I got my rough estimate – about $1000 dollars – much more than I was willing to spend and informed Candice. We negotiated for a few minutes and agreed to defer the project. In our house though, I never know if the "No" is a final agreement – or a starting point of a new negotiation. I'll only find out the extent of her persistence a day or so later if the negotiations start again.

The next day, I came downstairs to find Candice clipping coupons and Alex, tape measure in hand, running around to all the furniture in the kitchen measuring it.

"20 dollars," he hollered out.

He measured again, "14 dollars."

"10 dollars."

"30 dollars."

After 10 minutes of measuring everything, he stopped, looked up at me and says, "Too much money. It's too much money."

Candice hasn't mentioned the countertop upgrade since.

The Santa Trap

When Alex was very small, he inherited a family friend's bike. It was old, rusty, and worn – with threadbare tires from too many skid marks on the pavement and one too many spills upon the concrete scuffing up the handlebars. It was a bike that had seen many triumphs and joys – and probably one or two harrowing escapes.

Alex knew it was his bike hanging up on the wall. We discussed it many times. I told him that as soon as we got training wheels, he'd have his bike.

Over the summer I started a project – I was going to resurrect the dinged-up red bike and give it to Alex for Christmas. As I began adjusting and resuscitating the hero to his former glory, I kept careful tab of the parts I would need to replace. A half hour into the project – when the cost of the parts eclipsed the price of getting a brand new bike at the store, I appealed to a higher power.

"Oh Santa Claus?" I wondered aloud. "Alex wants a new bike."

And somewhere in the whirring emptiness of the internet, pleas were heard and duly recorded, box attached, and connected to a red and white receipt that looked remarkably like an archery target.

What? Santa doesn't deliver pre-assembled toys anymore?

Apparently not--and may never have--as my parents once told the story of how Santa's presents had gotten waylaid in an Eastern European country and arrived at the house in a box with "some assembly required" and directions in Polish. At least the elves who live in the far north speak many languages, making for easier translation. Santa's helpers set to work assembling the fire-engine red bicycle, carefully and strategically hidden to await the rest of the drop-shipped presents from the North Pole. When Alex awoke on Christmas morning, the new bike in all its brilliance was surrounded by a multitude of toys from Santa's workshop.

Alex saw the new bike and ran over to it, "Daddy, Daddy, Daddy, Santa brought the training wheels for my bike."

~@~

The Reluctant Gardner

There comes a time in early spring, when both flowers and humans emerge from their winter slumber and begin to bloom again. The days grow warmer necessitating the annual pilgrimage to the home and garden supercenter—or more often than not, multiple trips, as dads being dads always forget at least one critical component that is not discovered until all of the pieces are laid out on the grass.

If you think letting dads loose in a gadget superstore is dangerous, imagine what a wondrous world it is for an inquisitive three-year-old who wants (much like his dad) to try out every gizmo. Quite likely the reason we forget things is that we are so focused on not letting our child touch the chain saw, that we forget to pick up the rubber hose we went there for in the first place.

After the third trip with Alex in tow, I finally had all of the pieces of the garden jigsaw puzzle and could begin the fun part of actually planting the flowers. Alex was excited about helping in the garden, as his daycare class had been growing "jacky beanstalks" out of lima beans. He carefully dug each little hole with the trowel and gently placed the flower potting in their rightful place.

A half hour later, we wiped our brows from the beads of sweat and admired our handiwork. Alex beamed with pride. A neighbor strolled by and we began to chitchat. As we were talking, I felt a cold blast of ice water explode off my back.

Wheeling around, I encountered a full force stream of water from the garden hose right between the eyes. Unbeknownst to me while I was momentarily distracted, Alex had located the garden hose and like a football player celebrating a victory by dumping water on his coach, proceeded to soak me.

"Why you little..." I said, in between wiping the water off my face as I ran toward the hose. Alex looked up, flashed a wide smile which soon turned to an "uh-oh" expression as he saw his soggy father approaching, dropped the hose still spraying, and sprinted like a demon to the door. He got there a moment before I did and slammed it shut, locking me outside. I hollered and bellowed at him through the window, to which he just smiled even wider at me through the glass.

"Open this door now!" I shouted, the pool of water forming around my feet.

"Hi Daddy," he waved, clearly enjoying his prank.

"You open this door right now," I commanded, as I yanked and jiggled on the door handle, the laughter of the neighbor behind me burning in my ears.

"Hi Daddy," he said even more pleased with himself, his goofy grin getting larger and larger by each dripping second.

I remembered that the back door was unlocked, so I raced around to the garage. By the time I got inside, I had cooled off, (quite literally) so I grabbed a towel from the bathroom and rung out my clothes. Alex, having seen me enter the bathroom immediately tried to escape out the front door. Leaping, I blocked him.

I closed the door on him with a thud and said "Oh, no you don't. Not this time."

He looked up at me with chagrinned moon-pie eyes. "Hi ...Daddy" is all he said.

~@~

Car Fight

If you have ever been married, you have had this fight at least once in the car—where the driver and the passenger do not see eye-to-eye when circling a crowded parking lot. Both make judgment calls—"Is that car going out?" or stalking your prey by creeping up behind them as the other drivers meander to their car. Inevitably, it leads to friction as both have reasons for doing – or not doing – something—and neither is communicating the reasons why. A missed parking spot, or nearly clipping a car, is usually just enough to rupture the tense nature of finding a treasured spot into open warfare.

"Turn here. You missed a parking spot." (Eye roll) Seething foam bubbles linger in the corner of her mouth. "Why didn't you take it? Now we have to go around again?" (exhale). Meanwhile you're thinking that if you could only find some of that duct tape you store under the seat for any plethora of car-related emergencies, you would buy yourself enough momentary tranquility that you could think straight enough to find that empty parking spot. Of course that won't solve the problem – and will most definitely cause significantly more problems later on, but you're not thinking about the future—or anything beyond five minutes hence. You're thinking about finding that elusive parking spot NOW.

It was on our third time circling around the parking lot, punctuated by plenty of "Fine" and deep exhales thrown in here and there from the passenger seat, over the plethora of missed parking opportunities.

Alex, listening intently to the entire exchange, decided to pipe up, in a way that quite literally stopped the car dead in its tracks.

"Leave Daddy alone. He doesn't know how to park the car."

The tension broken, I slammed on the breaks and laughed. Pretty soon Candice and then Alex joined in and were rocking the car with laughter. Ignoring the cascade of car horns behind us as we blocked traffic, it suddenly occurred to me.

"Little Dude's got my back."

... and with that renewed confidence, not only did I find that valued parking spot, I "learned" how to park again, and quickly zipped into the stall before some other competitor could nose around me and steal my elusive jewel.

~@~

The Bike Ride

After nine years of marriage, Candice's bike had given up the ghost. Tired, worn, creaky—and never quite comfortable-- Candice dreaded that bruising contraption. The red beast was never a good fit for her, and we resolved that it was time to donate it. While perusing the local sporting goods store, she spied a shiny light blue touring bike staring back at her, enticing her with its newness and speed by which the brakes actually stopped the bike without leaving a stain of shoe leather on the tarmac.

From the moment she locked eyes to the reflectors, she was smitten--riding two or three times a week and dragging the family along. We even successfully made it 16 miles to the National Zoo (though we chickened out and hopped the metro back.) On the trails, she often powered ahead, while I lagged behind with a combined 50 pound bike seat and child lashed securely to the rear axle of a bicycle clearly not built with this in mind.

Going down the hills, the contraption grinded along, propelled by the extra velocity. On uphill climbs, the bike gasped, creaked, and wheezed like the cranky old relic it is, protesting loudly with a chain slip or two reminding me it didn't want to be used as mule train hauling freight. I knew if I was going to reach the top, I had to get out of the saddle and climb. Standing on the pedals, I ascended to the plateau. As I neared the halfway point, I hear a plaintive, urgent voice behind me. "DADDY I WANT TO RIDE ON MOMMY'S BIKE. YOURS IS TOO BUMPY!" and punctuated with a quick kick to the back of my upper thigh.

"Hey! That hurts" I yelled, more surprised than injured, as the kick broke my concentration mid-stride and rapidly decelerated the bike to a grinding halt. "Why did you do that?"

"The bike is bumpy when you stand. I want to ride on Mommy's bike."

It took me a few moments to think about what he said while I paused and caught my breath. Finally it dawned on me that when you stand tall in the saddle to gain momentum; those behind you get taken for a wild ride. Sometimes it takes a good swift kick in the pants for the leader to recognize that they have an obligation to ensure as little a bumpy ride as possible, lest the members of the caboose want to ride on Mommy's bike instead.

~@~

A Little TV

Lately I've been getting concerned about Alex's TV watching habits. It seems that every day he comes home from school; all he wants to do is turn on the TV and watch some shows. I know he has had a long day - even longer than ours --and that he's as tired as am I after working for 8 hours—but I don't like the TV on all of the time. Some days I don't fight it and he watches more than he should—but for the last few weeks it's been a running battle and I was determined to break the habit.

One day, I found an egg timer that was in our kitchen junk drawer

I walked over to where Alex had plopped himself on the couch and showed him the teakettle-shaped egg timer and set the time to 30 minutes. "Yesterday we said we were only going to watch a little TV. When the buzzer rings, we're going to turn the TV off," and then promptly placed it out of his outstretched arms reach.

After a few minutes of him reaching in vain for the timer, he resumed watching his show while I prepared dinner. At the conclusion of the show, the timer rang. I got up and turned off the TV. "We said a little TV tonight."

Alex looked at me, looked up at the TV and protested loudly. "HEYYYYYYYYYYYY. You said we could watch a *little* TV. This is the BIG TV. The *little* TV is in your room. Turn. The. TV. on. NOW." He huffed, deliberately driving his foot into the floor at the end of each word to emphasize his point.

I tried to explain that little was describing time not the size of the TV—but it is very hard to argue semantics with a toddler who's had his TV privileges revoked—and in his mind, very unfairly.

~@~

Coins in the Fountain

It was a crowded, bustling waterfront restaurant at Ghirardelli square in downtown San Francisco. Waitresses nimbly carrying trays of sundaes pirouetted through the tightly packed room. On more than one occasion, someone bumped into another, several people away – starting a chain reaction that usually ended up with the server teetering dangerously close to spilling the contents of her tray on top of us.

Alex did not like this jostling. He protested loudly to Candice about wanting to see the fountain outside. Candice, talking to her longtime friend of more than a dozen years, seemed oblivious to his pleas.

Taking that as my cue, I quickly slurped the rest of my sundae—generating the searing ice cream vapor lock in my brain and scooped Alex up to take him out to the fountain—a sculpture of a mermaid, resting on an island of rocks and coins flickering in the shallow ripples. Candice called nonchalantly after us, "Bring us back something sparkly."

Nursing my brain freeze headache, I handed Alex a couple of coins to keep him occupied. He leaned up to the waters edge and tossed them in one by one with a 'ker-plunk' and watching them flutter to the bottom.

"Oooo. Shiny," he called out. "Mommy likes shiny."

"Yes she does."

I glanced back at the door to see if Candice had come out yet. In the back of my freeze-fogged mind the muffled warning bells were just going off. I could hear his wheels turning. Subconsciously, I knew his next move. I looked back to see that he had climbed up and was nearly over the rock wall and intercepted him just before he tumbled in.

I pulled him out and asked him why he did it. "Mommy likes shiny," he said.

He was going fishing to get his mom a shiny bauble. Too bad he didn't know it wasn't his to take.

~@~

Snow Joke

Ever come up with a really funny joke that you just can't keep to yourself, and end up telling everyone within hearing distance the story? Pretty soon you've forgotten who you've told the joke to and friends of yours are spotting you a block away and pretending that they are on an important call with their boss when you walk by.

I have one of those rare moments every once in a while. Normally it takes my friends avoiding me for a week before I finally get the hint that maybe, just maybe, the first time they heard it, it was funny, but the second, third and fourth time, they are pained beyond belief.

Sometimes it takes the voice of a little person to put things back into perspective and realize just how annoying you are being – since none of your friends will be polite enough to call you on it. Instead, they nod silently, recounting their grocery list or desperately searching for anything to change the topic.

The winter of 2009-2010 so far had been the snowiest ever on record for the Washington, DC area. We actually had gotten more snow than Fargo, North Dakota. At one point in January to February, we had back-to-back, 100- year storms less than a week apart that dropped a combined 54 inches of snow on our front yard. The same week we had our storms, Canada was hosting the Olympics and it turned unseasonably warm— so warm in fact that they were trucking snow in from six hours away to keep the ski slopes frozen.

I remarked to my friend, "The Olympics called. They want their snow back." His laughter encouraged me a bit too much, and pretty soon I was re-telling everyone I knew. I think that I finally realized that I had said it a bit too often, as I picked up Alex from school and he tugged at the sleeve of a classmate's mother, repeating my line to her. For him it was hysterical, for me it was a blunt reminder that I had told the story enough and probably needed to find some new material.

~@~

Present Piggies

Ever since Alex was a baby, Candice has secretly enjoyed playing with his baby toes. She placed his foot in her hand and charted how it slowly grew from one barely the length of a finger, to one overshadowing the entire hand. Often she bonded with him by pretending to eat his piggies, gobbling them up to his squealish delight, kicking and giggling at the air. It was a ritual between him and her, just as the bedtime routines are a treasured habit between Alex and me.

Candice arrived home one night from work after a long, exhausting, and extremely frustrating day. I can usually tell from the moment she walks in by the first comment out of her mouth whether the day went well or not for her. Apparently Alex can too. When she spotted a toy out of place on the rug at 20 paces, I concluded that I should do my own thing that night.

Alex turned from the couch and intently watched Candice enter the room, taking off her jacket in a huff and disappearing upstairs to take a shower and remove the remains of the day, both mental and otherwise. As she climbed the first step Alex calls out, "MOMMY I'VE GOT A SECRET."

Candice paused and glanced over the banister, her scowling train of thought broken.

"MOMMY. I've got a SECRET. Come here Mommy.

Moooooooommmmmmmmmy, I SAID I've got a secret."

"Oh all right. What's your secret?" Candice verbalized, barely able to cover her annoyance and turned and started down the stairs.

Alex sat down on the rug facing Candice, strained and pulled his shoes off one by one and tosses them aside.

"Mommy, I've got a secret."

Candice reached the last step as Alex pulled off his socks and lay there with his feet dangling in the air.

"PIGGIES!!!!!!!!"

Immediately Candice's demeanor changed. She walked up to him played with his toes for a few moments and gave him a big, lasting hug. More than words, or other actions, Alex knew intuitively what Mom needed to feel better. It shattered her funk and restored her naturally sunny disposition.

14. Learning Moments

Why is it that the smallest thing will occupy a child's attention? They can be barreling around at top speed, but then something catches their eye stopping them dead in their tracks. Usually--much to the chagrin of Mom-- that fascinating object is an old wad of chewing gum, a pigeon dropping, or a rock with a slimy snail. It will occupy a child's inquisitive nature as they bend, and feel, and observe and watch in amazement at the slightest little changes.

Rocks, sticks, pebbles, flowers, tiny ponds accumulating at the end of a downspout—all are potential targets for the observing glances of a toddling one-year-old—which is wonderful when trying to figure out how something works—but works to our disadvantage when we're trying to get somewhere. The blocks of cement that have replaced my son's feet make it nearly impossible to pick him up and move him when he is focused on the conquest of his moment. It's as if the force of inquisitiveness is greater than our will to keep to a timetable. The world around him melts away - as he hyper-focuses on the object in front of him and ignores everything else—all while Mom is frantically rummaging through her purse trying to find the hand sanitizer.

~@~

Iguana

It's an age old tradition - 'What do you wear for Halloween?' that probably dates back to the Druids first use of the animal skins to scare away the evil spirits. ('Here child, son of star, wear the bear skin'... 'NO I wanna wear the leopard -it's faster and got more spots...')

And on it goes. Each act of defiance becomes a new generation's calling card. For us, the battle raged on between a red, furry monster and a green, scaly lizard.

We walked by a Halloween storefront - and Alex stopped and pointed at the Elmo costume in the window. He started jumping up and down shouting,"Elmo! Elmo! Elmo!" increasing, the tempo and insistence in his voice with each cadence.

Now as much as I really wanted to give in to his whims, I was not about to spend $39.99 on an outfit that was little more than a bath mat, so I said to him, "Elmo can't come home with you tonight. How about an iguana instead?" (We already had the scaly-looking towel at home—it was just a matter of reconfiguring it a bit.)

"Iguana"

"NO ... want Elmo," Alex said, pointing to the window.

"IG-uana" I repeated.

"NO ... ELMO," he exclaimed as he pressed both hands against the window pane.

"IGUANA" I urged, slightly raising my voice, and needlessly exacerbating the situation.

"ELMO! ELMO! ELMO!" he shouted, banging his hands on the glass for dramatic effect.

The debate raged as tenuously as you can possibly debate a one-and-a-half-year old—which is to really say - not a debate at all but a contest to see who can wail the loudest in 30 seconds or less.

He won the debate, but not the prize. I scooped him up over my shoulders and carried him kicking in the air before he could shatter the window separating him from the furry creature.

When we got home, I had an idea. I took out his favorite bedtime book from the diaper bag-- *I Wanna Iguana* and held it out to him. "What's this?" I asked.

He pointed at the book and said, "Iguana."

I pointed to the towel. "That's an iguana."

I pointed at the book – "Iguana." I pointed at the towel—"Iguana."

Then I put the towel on his head and pointed to him saying, "Iguana. Iguana. Iguana."

Later that night, we went trick-or treating, Alex wore his Iguana costume carrying his book for emphasis and clarification. We only lasted for a few minutes before Alex called it a night, returning home to greet the rest of the trick-or-treaters. Mom answered the door and soon she had a new helper. At each new ring of the doorbell, she would open and compliment the children on their costume: "That's an awesome costume," she'd say to each of the miniature Spidermen, pixie princesses and dwarfish swamp things. Alex chimed in, "Awesome. Awesome. Awesome."

Something changed, though, when the kids entered the house. Instead of handing out the candy to the costumed revelers, he began to horde it. After some convincing, he finally, reluctantly, parted with the goodies. Still, you could see his wheel turning as the next group of kids arrived.

No sooner had the kids stepped inside the house when Alex, still in his Iguana costume, grabbed the basket of candy nearly as big as he was and ran into the kitchen shouting, "MINE, MINE, MINE, MINE!"

As the green iguana lumbered down the hall lugging the basket, I motioned to the costumed cabal in my living room – "Hold that thought. Your candy just ran away," and raced down the hall to chase my son.

~@~

The Blanket Edge

Most of us remember a sight, sound, touch, or smell from our childhood that comforts us. It could be something as simple as the taste Mom's pumpkin pie fresh from the oven, or the crackling sound of leaves burning in the fall. For me, it was always the smell of a fresh pile of laundry, still warm from the dryer. I could take a deep breath of the clothing freshly imbued with the fabric softener and instantly feel I was safe in my bed.

It had been several months since Candice's father passed away, and she occupied her time on a Sunday morning by clipping coupons and doing housework to distract her from her loneliness. Normally, she would have been preparing to go spend some hours with him in his apartment, but now the click-click of the scissors hummed in rhythm and gave her other things to do as she got on with the business of living. Alex leaned his head on her arm as she cut out the rectangular squares.

Suddenly Alex had an idea. He reached over and handed his most treasured possession – his blanket --to Candice and said, "Smooooooooth."

Candice looked up from her task, perplexed.

Alex again repeated, "smooooooooth."

Candice raised her right eyebrow into an arch.

Alex leans over grabs Candice's hand and thrusts the corner of the blanket into the palm of her hand and says "smooooooooth" while rubbing the edge of the blanket.

We finally understood.

Alex was teaching us that his blanket had a smooth sateen edge, worn threadbare through many months of use. It was an edge that Alex had used to comfort himself many times—and he was showing Candice how to use the blanket to comfort her—as if the very presence of the blanket was enough to take all her cares away.

~@~

The Pirate Quilt

What began as a traipsing around on deck with a cardboard sword and a bandanna during one of our holiday cruises has turned into a full-fledged obsession with pirates. Pirate ships, pirate books, pirate flags, pirate hats, everything. He walks with a swagger and a blowup plastic sword saying "Aaaaargh Matey. Hoist the sails or walk the plank. AAAAAARGH!"

As part of his transition to his big boy bed, we took him to the store and let him pick out his bedding. It was not a big surprise that he chose a pirate-themed quilt and comforter. On one side, there was a treasure map, on the other, a series of islands on an azure blue sea with treasure chests, cannons and various sea creatures in between.

The night we brought his bedding home and assembled his new room, Alex took the cruise ship trophies that he won – one from each Carnival cruise -- and proceeded to sail them around the islands on the quilt. Later that night, as he was helping to clean his room and choosing which of his baby toys to give away to a family who lost everything in a fire, he went to his shelf and pulled down one of his trophies and handed it to Candice.

"Take my ship."

"Why do you want to give up your trophy?" Candice asked in return.

Alex thought pensively for a moment and blurted out with a compassion not often found in toddlers. "Not every boy can have a cruise ship. He can sail the islands with me."

~@~

Dessert Table Temptress

As a parent, I often hear myself saying, "Don't do this. Please do that. Put that figurine down," and any number of commands trying to instill some discipline in a young and pliable mind. Often I have my doubts that I'm being listened to. Like Jiminy Cricket's conscience, parental entreaties are nonchalantly brushed aside. We are but buzzing gnats in our children's ears.

I often lie awake wondering if Alex will remember to not put his hand on a hot stove, or do his chores without a fuss, or choose correctly between right and wrong....

...Actually that one I'm not too concerned about. Every time I do something slightly out of the established rules – he's always right there to correct me—so him following the rules isn't something that he'll have a problem with. It's peer pressure – what will he do when the cool kids are doing something they're not supposed to be doing.

One night in December, the three of us attended a Christmas party at a local restaurant. Early on, we set limits for Alex: chicken nuggets were OK, pizza squares were OK, but no sipping from Mom's brightly colored cocktail in a tall slender glass – (Not OK) launching his wind up airplane and matchbox cars off the table – (certainly NOT OK). Patiently, he abided by our wishes. We told him that if he was good, he could pick out one dessert at the end.

After the dinner service was completed, the dinner hostess brought out the dessert tray. Alex's eyes widened – on the tray were bite-sized cheesecakes – just large enough for a small nearly four-year-old to shove into his mouth without taking a bite. He asked politely if he could have some—and we told him that he had been a good boy all night and as a reward, yes he could have one. He unwrapped the paper and held in his hand, its gooey contents oozing out on his fingertips. His eyes lingered on the tray – and I could see the wheels turning in his mind.

A woman approached him. She was a late 40s blonde in a silver, sparkly-sequined top, with her hair done up very nicely. She was one of the hostesses, someone who left the details to others so that she could flitter about.

'Would you like another dessert?" she cooed to Alex. "How about two or three?" She said as her eyes shimmered reflections off her dress. "Your parents won't mind."

I watched him out of the corner of my eye, wanting to see what his reaction would be. Would he give in to the temptation, or would he follow through on what he had been told?

He looked longingly at the cheesecakes. You could see him puzzling it over. With a resolute jab he pointed to the one in his hand. "My mommy said I can have one."

Again the devil in glitter and bows countered. "I think you've been a good boy. Have another one," as she handed him a second.

Most children I know would have eaten that cupcake, but Alex handed it back to her. "My Mommy said I could have ONE"—and promptly handed it back to the hostess. Before she could try a third time, Alex stuffed his whole hand in his mouth with his one remaining cheesecake and walked away.

While I doubt that I could be that resolute with bite-sized cheesecake, I was silently very proud of him. He had stood up to very intense peer pressure – and from an adult no less—and knowing what was right, chose to walk away.

~@~

Snow Beam

Have you ever stopped to look at the world through the eyes of a child? Have you ever sat in wonder at a rainbow and watch it spread across the window of a car? Have you ever looked up and watched the shapes in the clouds as your parent drives from place to place? For adults, it is about the destination, for children, it is about the journey.

It was an ordinary day in December where the world seemed still and at peace. The "Shopper-stopper" blizzard from the previous weekend was piled high everywhere the eye can see. Mountains of natural mazes in white- and we the humans and cars, the mouse, in search of an exit.

As is often the case, what man builds, nature destroys, as if to obliterate the scars of man from an otherwise perfect world. The pile of snow reached higher than the pumps at the gas station, where it had been pushed by the plow. Nature began its work chipping away at the edifice. Already it had carved out the side where the sunbeams hit, forming a crest like a Santa hat, lop-eared and fluffy, leaning on one side.

Alex gazed longingly out the window as I filled the car up with gas. He focused intently on the thin walls of the snow peak with the sunlight streaming through. In a voice of wonder only a three-year-old can ask, he looked at me and inquired, "Why does some of the snow melt but not others?"

I thought of explaining nature, that the warm rays melt from the outside in. I thought of describing the sunbeam as a laser that God uses to put holes in the snow. Instead I wondered aloud that I didn't rightly know, why one sunbeam would choose a flake and not the one below.

I stood there pumping the gas, and we talked as the car filled up. I asked him the questions of what he might rightly know. We both came up with hypotheses - some far-fetched and wild-eyed. Perhaps a monster bit the candy cone from the side. Too soon, the task was done, and off we journeyed again - but the memories of his inquisitiveness will linger on, long after that last melting snowflake has liquefied and gone.

~@~

15. Outsmarted!

Parents say one thing. Children hear another. Often the very words we say are turned against us by beings who take meanings very literally. At three years of age, all children become lawyers, and can out-argue the most seasoned diplomat.

For us, the battle of the wills started much earlier than that one Easter Sunday morning when he was about 14 months old. The three of us were in the kitchen while Candice prepared breakfast. Alex pointed at the Cheerios box on the countertop and was making a fuss about wanting to eat them on the rug. Candice walked over to his high chair and poured a handful on the tray, picked him up, and put him in his seat. After eating several Cheerios, he stopped, defiantly looked us square in the eyes, grasped a small handful and tossed them on the floor.

The rule in our house is food getting tossed means that you're finished your meal and you are excused from the table. So we picked him up out of his high chair, and set him down on the rug. He promptly toddled back into the kitchen, scooped the Cheerios one by one off the floor from under his high chair, and hop-skipped back to the rug. He plopped down on the rug and shoved the fistful of cereal into his mouth, grinning happily.

I looked up from the morning newspaper and turned to Candice, "You do realize that we've just been played by a one-year old?"

Remind me never to play chess with him as he gets older.

~@~

Pushing Buttons

It was day eight of the parents being held hostage. Sometime earlier the previous week—the exact days are blurry because—well, we haven't slept since before I can remember. The reason for THIS sleep deprivation would be a small little object with buttons, a toddler's curiosity and a hiding place so secret, no parent can ever find it.

Candice uses a stopwatch for work– it is necessary for her to be able to tell the exact time to the partial second a particular video clip runs. Alex found this stopwatch, and proceeded to play with the buttons.

All would be well and good – except that he has now activated the alarm to go off every 24 hours – AT

THREE-AM-IN-THE-GOSH-FORSAKEN MORNING. He then hid said stopwatch in our bedroom in a place that neither of us can find. Every morning at exactly 3:00 AM, the alarm goes off for exactly three minutes – and then goes silent. It's just long enough to wake you from a deep sleep but not long enough to wake up, stagger out of bed to find the blasted thing and beat it within an inch of its life—mainly because we DON'T KNOW WHERE IT IS. For the entire week, I woke up to this "beep beep bebeeeep"— jump out of bed to kill it and cannot locate it -- then lie awake in bed for at least the next hour trying to think of all the places it could be hidden because now I'm obsessed about this small plastic contraption. By the time I finally get back to sleep – the REAL alarm clock is going off in my head and now I'm ready to throw *IT* through the wall.

I've tried to be nice, I've begged and pleaded with Alex, "Please, PLEEEEEASE tell daddy where you put the stopwatch." But the answer never comes.

On day ten—long after I capitulated—I finally found the stopwatch – which, incidentally, was hidden inside a box, inside a drawer pulsing like Edgar Allen Poe's *Tell-Tale Heart*. The only reason I discovered it, was because I methodically searched the entire room from corner to corner, undoing cabinets, boxes, drawers until I located it. As I restored the room, Alex found a new "toy" to torture us with.

Alex picked up the house alarm keychain, activated it in immediate response mode—and then sat it back down on the table where it had been resting. His trap set, he quietly resumed playing with his toys on the floor. As I passed by, he innocently asked, "Juice, please." Being the kind, naïve, father that I am, proceeded to go downstairs and get him a cup of juice.

About half way down the stairs, I broke the alarm beam sending 100 decibel sirens wailing throughout the house. Taken by surprise, I stumbled down the remaining steps, tripping over at least three strategically placed toys in my walking path, and careened into the kitchen wall with a dull thud and a frustrated exhale. Cursing and muttering, I finally made it to the alarm and disabled it.

Grudgingly, I grabbed Alex's juice off the shelf in the refrigerator and started back up the stairs. Halfway to the first landing, I hear another alarm going off. Alex had gotten hold of my keys and set off another cascade of sirens in our car with the panic button. I raced up the stairs. Alex greeted me with a sly, knowing smile, and gladly reached out saying, 'Juice please," as if nothing had happened.

I would be looking for the candid camera hidden somewhere in the house, but I'm certain that it is a waste of time. If it was there, Alex has already re-hidden it.

~@~

The Toddling Houdini—Part I

I'm thoroughly convinced that my son must have been a magician in a previous life, or at least Houdini's brother, because he always manages to escape from something confining him.

One day while I was cooking dinner, I had given him a plate of grapes to keep him occupied and strapped him into the booster seat attached to our kitchen chair. As I was boiling the water for the tortellini, I glanced back over to where Alex was sitting. Alex was no longer sitting in his chair but standing on the seat.

Now, I knew I had strapped him in before I made dinner, so I thought maybe I just hadn't buckled him in properly. 'Maybe the strap became loose?' I wondered. So I went over to sit him back down in his chair. The strap was still connected at both legs.

I looked down, and noticed that the back of the fold up booster seat was removed, lying on the floor a few feet from where the chair stood. The seat was intact when I sat him in it. "What could he have done to get out of the seat?" I thought.

I put the booster seat back together and re-strapped him in. A few minutes later, I brought the dinner over to the table—and again the seat back was hanging ajar. I stood there for the next two minutes holding the dinner plate as Alex proceeded to rock the booster seat back—forward -back and forward one last time, and then finally out of the track, disdainfully disposing of it as it clattered to the floor. He leaned backwards almost horizontally through the hole in the back and began to inch his foot out of the restraints. Once he had one foot clear of the restraints, he used that foot to push the rest of his body out of the harness.

With a look of immense satisfaction befitting the magician that he was, he stood up in the chair and began to clap for himself.

There will not be another death-defying escape from the booster seat. I picked him up, set him down on the floor, and promptly retired the booster seat for good. The curtain opened and fell on the toddling Houdini, before he too, could fall.

~@~

The Toddling Houdini—Part II

All parents take short-cuts: whether it is reading the beginning and ending of a book that you've read a thousand times so you can wrap up bedtime quickly, or throwing chicken nuggets in the microwave instead of cooking a freshly prepared meal. Anyone who says otherwise, is lying.

One such shortcut we made was putting hair twisties on the cabinet doors instead of purchasing those complex-hard-to-open-even-for-a-parent-designed-by-Ft.-Knox-security-guard cabinet locks. We've been told many times that if you twist them tight enough, they're so strong that little kids can't get into them. The inventor of that little nugget of conventional wisdom, alas, has never met Alex.

Alex could be playing with blocks across the room or doing just about anything ordinary—yet his actions are really just a cover story. He's actually conducting espionage—probing our defenses and waiting for the right moment to strike.

One night, after successfully discovering that chairs are not just for sitting on—they can also be used to obtain chocolates stored in a bowl in the center of the dining room table—he realized that the evidence of his trespass littered the floor like a roadmap to a guilty burglar. So he did what most spies do: he covered his tracks.

Alex bent down, picked up the shredded pieces of aluminum candy wrappers, and bundled them in a ball. Nonchalantly, he strolled into the kitchen to the cabinet where the trashcan is kept and disabled the "kid-proof" hair twisty, tossed in the aluminum confetti, and stealthily replaced the twisty on the door before strolling away.

'Did we leave the cabinet open by mistake?' I wondered. I didn't think so. The next night I watched him repeat his feat, confirming that the first time was not a fluke—he had indeed cracked the "cabinet code."

~@~

Juice with Dinner

Candice and I had been openly fretting over how much juice Alex drinks. Even though we water it down, we cannot get him to drink water or milk "straight up." There always has to be a flavor for it—and I think we've established really bad precedent by being so lax with the rules.

One day at daycare, another parent offered a suggestion: 'Institute a rule that juice can only be drunk at meal time—and that he drinks water the rest of the time.'

'What a great idea,' I thought, and went home that evening to implement this new rule. I sat Alex down on the chair and told him, we have a new rule "Juice only during dinner time," and explained to him that we would drink water afterwards.

We finished dinner and were playing with the toys in the den. Alex asked for more juice. I told him "No—we're going to drink water now. Juice is for dinner time."

Alex looked up at me, pondered for a moment and opened the door to his cabinet, rummaging around for something. He emerged with one of his plates. Alex marched over to the table, pulled himself up on his chair, put the plate down in front of him and turned to me. "Dinner time! Juice Please!"

And with that, my ingenious plan was dashed to smithereens. I'd been outsmarted by my two-and-a-half year old. Curses! Foiled again!

~@~

That's a game, not a book.

Every night before bed, Alex and I read at least one book. When he doesn't want to go to bed yet, he introduces a variety of stalling tactics. One night, it is wanting to pick his pajamas out, another it's bringing his step stool over and playing with the light switch. Lately though, his favorite game tends to be wanting to play a board game or do a puzzle before bed. The first couple of times he succeeded—but now that I know how long it takes to play the game, I have banished it from our nightly routine.

Alex knows this, which is why nearly every night for the last week he's tried to get me to play a game with him. Rather than hear the wrath of Mom, who after listening to stalling tactics for about a half-hour will usually shout – 'ALEX-BEDTIME –NOW!'—and it's usually directed at me, not at him.

"Come on Alex, time for bed."

"I want to play a game. Can we play Candy Land?"

"No we can't play CandyLand. CandyLand is a game, not a book. Pick out a book."

"Can we play shoots and ladders?"

"No we can't play Chutes and Ladders. Chutes and Ladders is a game, not a book. Pick out a book."

"Can we play fishy game?"

"Fish game is a game, not a book. Please pick out a book."

"Can we play Curious?" referring to a motorized Curious George on a banana that travels around a track that you can configure yourself. He says that as he moves in for the kill, a secret smile barely visible upon his face.

"No we can't play Curious George. Curious George is a game, not a book. Pick out a book."

"No it's not. Here's Curious George. SEE!" With that, he walks over to his bookshelf and pulls out his Curious George book and hands it to me with a grin bigger than his face.

I had been set up, volleyed, and spiked.

~@~

Figuring It All Out

Toddlers are very adept at using subterfuge. They may not yet know right from wrong, but can definitely stretch the truth enough to fit their own objectives. They have carefully memorized the nuances of any rule and use each against you as they see fit.

What do you do when two incompatible rules collide? I was raised that you do not leave the table until everyone is done, that if you start a meal together, you should end a meal together, and rarely should one leave the table before everyone is finished eating. One evening, as we were visiting family, we tried to pass those values along to the next generation. Alex asked to be excused from the table, and his smile turned into a frown when his request was denied. You could see him stewing and ruminating about his predicament—until suddenly his eyes brightened and he shouts out, "Daddy I have to go potty"—which in our house grinds everything to a halt and we rush him to the nearest potty to reinforce his continued success. He had used the one thing he knew would get a reaction out of us—his potty trump card. I took him to the bathroom, only to be greeted by a mischievous grin leaning over his shoulder and a small voice quietly saying to me as he batted his eyes, "Daddy, I don't have to potty. Can I leave the table, pleeeease?"

"Batting your eyes may work for your mother but it doesn't work for me. Back to the table." I responded—though secretly even as I heard the words coming out of my mouth, knew, like a genie escaping from a bottle, that getting him back in his seat at the dinner table would require multiple applications of bungee cords, duct tape and crazy glue.

~@~

Monster Shoes

Kids' shoes are not like adult shoes. They are cheap, poorly put together, and worn through so fast that by the time the child outgrows them, their next and final destination is a landfill. We're lucky if we can get 1-2 seasons out of them at best.

Alex's Thomas the Train shoes had seen better days and Candice had taken him to the store as a reward for good behavior and allowed him to pick out a pair of shoes. He walked over to the racks and pulled out what can only be described as monster shoes - camouflaged plastic gardening slip-on shoes that were all the rage a couple years back and decorated with superhero and swamp thing buttons.

Candice winced. They were truly some of the most hideous shoes we had ever seen. "Here's a pair of loafers. Can you try them on instead?" In her hands she held a pair of brown and white hush-puppies—equally hideous to a boy, but perfectly sensible and acceptable to a stylish mom.

"No, I want the monster shoes," he stated, thrusting them demandingly at Candice.

"I don't like those shoes, go pick out another pair," she countered.

The two of them squared off like cagy boxers circling on the mat, neither one willing to budge. Finally after about 5 minutes of continual eye contact, Alex blinked first – or at least seemed to.

He walked back to the shelf, picked up the pinkest, sparkliest, glitteriest pair of shoes that exist in the universe and marched back to mom. "I want THESE," he stated with a self-impressed smirk.

Candice took one glance at the pink sparkle shoes, sighed heavily, looked around to make sure no one was watching and said, "Oh, all right, you can have the monster shoes." As Alex returned the sparkle shoes to the shelf, a thin smile cracked out of the side of his mouth. He triumphantly held the monster shoes aloft— the boxer claiming his title belt.

~@~

Y-7

We were visiting Alex's cousins and were trying to find some cartoons to entertain the kids while the parents talked. Scanning through the list of shows, we passed one cartoon on the dial that was a little cruder than is rightfully appropriate for the under-five crowd. Indeed, as the warning rating in the upper left corner indicated, the program about a certain yellow spongy character was geared for children at least seven years old.

Alex's cousin, older by just two years, wanted to watch the show—but only by himself. He didn't want to be hassled by all of the smaller kids. Using the rating as an excuse, he pointed at the screen and said, attempting to chase away the younger watchers, "This show isn't for little kids to watch - it's only for kids older than seven."

That may have worked on his younger sister, but it didn't work on Alex. Alex challenged his older cousin, "You're not seven." (Correctly I might add—since his cousin was nearly six and shouldn't have been watching it either by his own standard.) At three-and-a-half, my son had used facts and logic to blow a hole in his older cousin's gambit to keep the TV all to himself.

~@~

But Why???

While walking to the grocery store one day with Alex, I learned a valuable lesson: If you don't know the answer, don't wing it and make something up—for my

Dad Desperately In Need of Training Wheels

three-year-old son has a mind like a steel trap, capable of remembering any small detail. I think I'll have him negotiate all my contracts from now on.

Dad: "Alex, get out of the middle of the road."

Alex: "But Why?"

Dad: "Because there's a car coming."

Dad: "Ok, It didn't turn down the alley."

Alex: "But Why?"

Dad: "Because it was going to go visit someone."

Alex: "But Why?"

Dad: "Because he was going to visit his Grandmom." I fudged as there is no way I could know why the car turned into a particular driveway. My purpose was to get him out of the road, not sing, *'Over the River.'*

Alex: "But Why?"

Dad: "Because his Grandmom is sick." (At this point, I'm already into the rabbit hole, so I'm trying to find my way out of it. Nothing is popping in my head.)

Alex: "But Why?"

Dad: "Because she ate something that wasn't right."

Alex: "But Why?"

Dad: "Because she needs her medicine?

Alex: "But Why?"

Dad: "Because she's not feeling well."

Alex: "But Why?"

Dad: "Because she misses her grandson."

Alex: "Ooooooooooooh"

Alex: "I hope she feels better."

Dad: "So do I."

Alex: "Does she make buttered noodles for her grandson?"

Dad: "I'm sure she does."

Three days later—long after I had forgotten the fiblet — the three of us were walking through the development when Alex asked where the noodle lady was and was she feeling better. "The noodle lady?" Candice asked puzzled, shooting me an arched eyebrow glance.

"Daddy said the noodle lady needed her medicine. Her grandson was bringing it to her."

I ducked the dagger eye thrown in my direction, "Yes, she is doing much better."

As I squirmed through the answer, I re-learned a valuable lesson: That it is far better to say you don't know the answer, than to open your mouth and remove all doubt.

~@~

Locksmith

About the same time that Alex grew tall enough to reach the garage door opener, he also discovered he had another skill – that of a locksmith. Within a week, he had successfully unlocked most of the doors in the house, and the ones that remain – well, either they don't interest him or it is only a matter of time before they too, fall.

One Sunday morning, Candice had gone off to the grocery store, and I was puttering around the house nursing my first cup of caffeine—weaving in and out of the maze of toys in the kitchen. I'd trip over one, mutter, and put it back in its toy box, only to trip on another one and grudgingly return to the place I had just left.

Alex, sensing my distraction, took the opportunity to try his new skills on the back door. Deftly he unlocked the door and headed out into the back yard--- only the Beep-Beep-Beep of the alarm alerted me to his departure.

I wheeled around and caught a glimpse of his foot as he sauntered out the door. As I made it to the door, I heard the whiir-whiirrrr-whiiirrrr of the garage door opener and my son making a break out the opening. Running and leaping down the steps, I caught him just as he was sprinting down the short driveway into our back alley. Scooping him up, I carried him back inside – locking the door to the garage from the inside to prevent a recurrence of the great escape.

About 10 minutes later, long after I had forgotten about the first transgression, and resumed reading the Sunday paper, Alex grabbed my keys off the countertop and strolled out the door for a second time. I followed him at a distance to see what he would do, ready to spring into action if he succeeded. Part of me was betting he would do it, the other part of me was betting he would see me first before completing his mission, so I hid behind a tree. I watched him try the door handle. Locked. Alex then tried each key, methodically, until he found the right key on the keychain. He turned the handle and off he strode triumphantly into the garage.

I then faced a quandary: Do I give him the momentary satisfaction of accomplishment, for having overcome the obstacles I placed in his path, or do I intercept him before he runs away. Ultimately, my decision was made for me, as again I heard the whiir of the garage door going up. I emerged from my hiding place, scooped him up a second time, put the keys in my pocket and again locked the door while bringing him back inside the house.

Five minutes later, I watched him rise from his toys, and retrieve the SPARE set of keys from its hiding place, that I thought was well-hidden (apparently not), exit the door and go back to work on the lock.

Outclassed and out-thought, I slipped on my shoes and took Alex for a walk. If he was going to escape—he should at least have his dad walking beside him.

16. Life Lessons

A couple of years ago, the Washington Post reported that a world-class violinist visited Washington DC incognito, and played several pieces by Bach for pocket change. Would anyone pause, or would they hurry by? Sadly, just a handful of passengers stopped to listen. The only ones who seemed to hear were the small children, who stopped a few moments before they were yanked away by their guiding hand. Somewhere along the way, we adults have lost the ability to listen, wrapped up in the million thoughts of our day-to-day lives, missing the simple sweetness of life.

One night, Alex, Candice, and I went out to dinner. In the foyer of the restaurant, a piano player was performing a classical piece, his fingers dancing on the keyboard like marionettes pulled tight by a string. The music was soft and barely uplifting—hardly "important" enough to remember, yet still the piano player labored on—his only appreciation—the occasional side glance of a patron on the way to the dining room and his own joy at plying his craft.

As we walked into the room, Alex froze, transfixed, still as a statue. Nothing could persuade him to move from that spot—no games, no distractions, and no new and exciting toys. As the piano man completed the last few notes of his song, 18 month old Alex began to wildly clap in appreciation.

The song that all of the adults in the room had missed, the little child had heard and it filled his heart with joy.

We all have places to go, but sometimes it takes a child to remind us to take a moment and listen.

~@~

Raspberry Water Delivery

It was mid-summer and the grocery stores were stuffed with fresh fruits and vegetables. I stopped by and picked up a number of items to encourage Alex to try new tastes. Some of them he liked (kiwi), others he didn't (plums). Still others, he could not get enough of—raspberries. He pushed a chair over to the countertop to climb up and grab handfuls of raspberries from the container, plopping down in his little chair to eat them.

The first few times, I paid attention to him—but after a few minutes of watching, the routine became commonplace, so I resumed preparing dinner.

Little did I know, that he had shoved every berry in his mouth and stealthily wandered out of the room into the dining room.

Every parent gets these premonitions – when the room is too quiet for some strange reason and all of the animals have gone into hiding. And when you get those premonitions—you immediately put everything down and go find your child – because inevitably, that's the time they're getting into trouble.

I turned the corner into the dining room. There, I found the disgorged remnants of the raspberries, having now been smeared into a large bloody arc on the beige carpet.

Muttering, I asked Alex why he did it, which Alex, being two-years-old, didn't respond—and I really didn't expect him to. Frustrated, I turned off the dinner on the stove and began cleaning up the mess.

If you've never tried to clean raspberries out of a rug, well let's just say the only thing I've ever tried to clean up that was more difficult than that was chocolate sauce—as the juice and the seeds conspire to permanently dye the carpet fibers flaming red—and no amount of scrubbing—no matter how vigorous—can get the stains out.

About 20 minutes into my scrubbing, Alex reappears into the dining room, tentatively peering around the corner. In his hands he held a cup of water that he had poured himself from the faucet in the sink.

"Here Daddy," he said.

I left the now light pink stains on the rug, got up, and hugged him. The stains are barely visible, but still there, reminding me every day of the love of a little boy who, of his own volition, tried to make amends.

~@~

Compassion

The other day I was watching Alex in the jungle gym area of the local mall while Candice ran some errands. Inside the play land were about 15 kids of varying ages, along with the approximate requisite number of parents—mostly Moms. Many of the parents were sitting on the benches lining the edges—engrossed in their own conversations and not paying much attention to their kids. Every once in a while, a small curly-haired head would pop out from the airplane shaped clubhouse and shout 'Mommy!' and wait for the anticipated response. Inevitably one of the parents would chirp up "over here [insert name of kid] and the child would get a big smile on their face and resume playing.

One tussle-haired boy about three years old, poked his head out of the cockpit seat and called out to his Mom. Mom, who was gabbing away on her cell phone didn't answer right away. He called out again. Still no answer.

The boy panicked. He started frantically looking around in the sea of parents and not seeing his mom launched into hysterics, bordering on hyperventilation.

With tears running down his reddening cheeks and a snot bubble forming in his nose, he attracted the sideways gaze of just about every parent in the room—except for the one who should have responded first, but was still blathering away on the cell phone oblivious to everything going on around her.

No one moved from their chairs. Alex poked his head out of the airplane to figure out what the commotion was all about. I watched him as he wandered over to the boy and offered him his toy train to play with, mostly to stop the very loud wailing. He distracted the boy long enough to stop crying. In the start-stop-start in between his tears, Alex managed to say to the boy, "Don't cry. Mommy be back soon." He knew that the quickest way to calm the boy's fears (and silence the ringing headache in his own head) was to assure him that his mom was nearby and would be right back. While I was sad, and mildly irritated that the mother never noticed the whole interaction from meltdown to resolution, I was proud of my son for stepping up, when no other child or parent would or could do so.

~@~

Blue... and "Other Blue"

Every time Alex's Grandy comes to visit from San Francisco, she brings him another blue sateen blanket from Pottery Barn. We now have three that we keep in rotation to allow them to get equally worn. He loves that blanket – he takes it to bed, he takes it on trips, he talks to it—it's probably his best friend.

On her most recent trip east, Grandy couldn't make it to Pottery Barn, so she stopped at a different store and picked up a new blue plush blanket. It certainly LOOKED the same—but somehow, it just doesn't feel quite the same. It didn't have the same smells, or the same touch—and Alex knew it. At first he was excited to have it – he had TWO Blue blankets—but after a few minutes he put the new one aside. It was relegated to the bottom of the crib, disdainfully tossed aside as "Other Blue."

Nowadays, he still requires "Other Blue" to be in the bed with him. He'll complain when "Other Blue" isn't there to keep him company. Even though "Other Blue" is more plush, more luxurious, and warmer, it is a second-class citizen in the kingdom crib—it never gets snuggled with between the thumb and curled up finger of the infant fast asleep.

When you meet "*the one*" you just know it—and no one else can take his, her – or its —place.

Eventually, though, our carefully structured charade of the rotating Blues was bound to be discovered. One day Alex was walking down the hall, dragging his blue blanket behind him and Candice was unloading the dryer. As he passed, he saw a freshly cleaned blue blanket still steaming, coming out of the dryer with the pile of laundry. He stopped and clenched his blanket tighter and watched Mom carry the load into the bedroom for folding and drop them in a heap. Quick as a wink, Alex ran in and grabbed the 2nd Blue Blanket—

spiriting it away to his own room. 'Blue' had a TWIN. Alex was confused.

He looked the newcomer over. It looked like his Blue blanket. Unlike "Other Blue", it smelled, and felt like his blanket—it WAS his blanket—but now there were TWO of them.

For the next few minutes he sat there, visibly distraught. "My Blue" he said, pulling one closer—then switching thumbs and saying "My Blue" again and clenching the other blanket. I watched Alex as he alternated thumbs in his mouth—first one, than the other, not entirely sure what to make of this new addition from the dryer duplicator.

In time, he resolved his own dilemma by making sure that BOTH blues go to bed with him. What will he do when he discovers there is still a third in hiding?

~@~

Daycare and Taxes

One day a year, two of life's certainties - daycare and taxes - collide. The third- death- might come about if I don't stop working myself into a frenzy over this taxes thing.

I use tax preparation software to do my taxes—it's worth the investment to maximize our deductions and legally minimize our taxable income. Every year, I dutifully itemize, compile, categorize, and record all of our expenses— it never ceases to amaze me how quickly this stuff adds up.

I close my office door, and don't come out until it's done—the weight of the world lifted off my shoulders. This was the first year I could deduct daycare expenses from my return.

I reached the end of the review and generally pleased with myself, began to check my work. An error message appeared about the daycare expenses – one of several discrepancies I had to correct before moving on. I'd seen many of them before – state and local taxes, for 401Ks, etc—but this was a new one blinking ominously at me.

I opened it up—and it says:

[Dollar amount] seems large. Are you sure?

I looked at the number on the screen- and the amount was correct as to what I calculated. I tried to click "Continue."

Again the error message popped up – mocking me— as if to say that I was a fool who deserved condescension for paying so much for daycare. It was more condescension than I could handle coming from a seemingly unintelligent machine.

Two floors below, Candice heard me shouting and rushed upstairs—expecting to find a bookshelf had fallen over or something. Instead she found an incoherent husband frothing at the mouth and babbling something about it not being 1950 anymore, that the computer had obviously never had children and never will as long he had anything to say about it, and that daycare providers in

Washington, DC can charge a king's ransom because there's so few of them and so many of us.

After a few more minutes of mouthing off. I calmed down took a deep breath and huffed at Candice:

"You do realize we spent more in daycare this year than I spent in my first year of college and this [Expletive deleted] computer thinks I'm a fool for doing so."

~@~

17: Father / Son Moments

Pop-Pop's Shoes

Many years ago, when I left home for my first job in the big city, my father gave me a pair of shoe-trees to keep my shoes looking new. It was the same pair of shoe trees that he had salvaged from his own father's meager possessions as he bid his house good bye to live with his Aunt and Uncle in Baltimore after his mom's passing. At age 17, he and his younger sister were both orphans.

Throughout the years, whenever I got a new pair of shoes, the shoe trees migrated from the old to the new, doing a much better job at protecting the shoes than I was doing polishing them.

One day Dad called, and wanted the shoe trees back. The newer ones he had bought just stretched the leather out too much. He wanted to reconnect with the old shoe trees –probably like he was reconnecting with the memory of his father from so long ago. Reluctantly, I pulled them out of my own shoes and set them aside to take to my parents' house.

The next night Alex found the shoe trees, at the foot of the bed. He liked watching them bend and flop – like a wooden marionette's shoe. He walked them across the floor, up the steps, down the steps, marching them around on the terracotta tile floor: clop-step, clop-step.

A few weeks later – after we had gone and visited my parents and returned the shoe trees to my dad, I looked at the shoe trees I now had in its place. Instead of metal—flimsy plastic. Instead of a solid block of wood – a pressboard mold. I marveled at how well the previous ones had been made, and how much quality had decreased with these later models.

Alex noted it too. He picked up the new shoe trees, held them up to me with a confused look on his face and asked:

"Where's pop-pop's shoes?"

~@~

Pop Pop's Medicine

On Saturday morning, December 20, Candice's father passed away. He had been deteriorating for a while but everything accelerated since his strokes 3 weeks earlier. We met with hospice on Friday night after they indicated that he had about a week left, and ten hours later, he was gone.

As his final wish, we celebrated his life at his favorite restaurant. Upon leaving the restaurant, we headed home in silence as we quietly reflected our own thoughts. Alex, in his car seat, piped up:

"Pop-pop's sick?" [Not to be confused with my father, also known as Granddad. At one point, all of the grandfather figures, Granddad (mine), Pop-pop (Candice) and Chief (Candice's Step-Father) were all Pop-Pop.]

"Yes Alex, Pop-pop's sick."

"When Alex is sick – take medicine."

"Yes Alex, when you're sick you take medicine to make you well."

"Alex take medicine, all better."

"Alex give Alex's medicine to Pop-Pop —make him all better."

Even though we had tried to shield him from all that was going on, Alex, as perceptive as he is, had figured it out on his own. In his mind everything, even death, could be solved with Alex's medicine. He was going to cure Pop-Pop's brain cancer with the medicine tube that had made him well again.

~@~

Shower Time

I sound like a broken record. Every morning when Alex wakes up, we ask him "Do you have to go potty." Every night before bed we ask him again, "Do you have to go potty?" It must just be the very act of thinking about it that finally reaches the brain – because inevitably, 5-10 minutes after we ask the question, he's filled to the brim and does the jiggle shuffle dance to the bathroom.

Day in, day out, for two months now, we've been going through this scene. I wonder silently to myself, "Will this routine ever end???" Must all toddlers be taught to perform a basic bodily function that we all take for granted?

And then one day the light bulb switched on. I was already in the shower when he woke up, after a night of sniffling and sneezing his way through a springtime cold. Alex knew that the warmth of the shower would open up his nose and make him feel better, so he ran down the hallway to our bathroom, stripped off his clothes and asked, "Daddy, can I take a shower with you?"

I leaned out of the door, the steam escaping through the slit and filling the room with a cloudy haze. "Of course you can. Did you go potty first?" He runs to the stall and yells out, "All finished."

"I didn't hear a flush."

<flush> "I did it."

"Ok, now you can come into the shower," I said as I opened the door wide, letting little water droplets congeal on the tile floor.

Alex runs into the shower and holds up his hands "pick me up"

I scooped him up and rested his head on my shoulder, swaying him slowly back and forth under the undulating pulse of the showerhead. Every time I moved slightly out of the stream he lifted his head up and looked at me with his contented eyes. "More Water," he commanded. I stood there thinking that this is what fatherhood was all about.

~@~

The Staying in Bed Blues

Size belies the truth. Our child is getting older. As much as our mind still sees Alex as a baby coming home from the hospital, or taking his first steps, etc., he is very much a little boy and no longer a baby.

Every night for three weeks straight, we put Alex to bed, and every night he crawls up between us to go to sleep, long after we have closed our own eyes. I don't know how he manages it, but he is so quiet, so stealthy, (or we're just too tired) that he never disturbs the covers as he climbs in—and then proceeds to nudge both of us out of our warm spots.

I've tried reading to him, tucking him in and sleeping on the floor next to him, waking up in the middle of the night and marching him back to his room. Nothing was working. So we did what others have done before us—and called in reinforcements. We tried several suggestions, but none of them worked, until offhandedly, one of Candice's co-workers suggested, "maybe he's outgrown his bed?"

'Outgrown his bed... how can that be?' I thought to myself. 'He's still a .... He's still a... baby.'

"You sure?"

That night I watched him as he slept in his toddler bed. I hovered over him waiting for him to stretch out—and sure enough, when he raised his arms, he whacked the headboards. Even with his arms by his side, he only cleared the head and footboard by less than six inches.

Somehow without our noticing it, our little baby had grown up. Later that weekend when we purchased a new big boy twin bed for him, did we come to the heartbroken realization that Alex wasn't crawling into bed with us because he needed our nighttime warmth. He crawled in because he needed room to grow. Since the very first night he slept in his own bed, he rarely returns to our bed. Still I secretly miss the toes in my back walking through the illusion that he wanted to be close to us.

~@~

Spiders and Jumping Bugs

When I was a boy about three years old, I would awake in the middle of the night with horrible nightmares about a jack-in-the-box, ready to pop out of the box and clamp onto my foot unwilling to let go. I'd jump out of bed and run down the hall into my parents' room to cower under the covers. Sometimes they'd let me stay. Usually though, my dad would escort me back to my room. I could never understand why he'd make me face my fears alone. Eventually I outgrew those fears, but I never quite trusted the Jack-in-the-Box after that. You know—just in case it came to life like the *Chuckie* movies of my adolescence.

I'm starting to see signs that Alex has the same nightmares I had as a child—but for different reasons. His fears center on jumping bugs and spiders. Every night lately, he tells me as he is getting ready for bed, that he's scared of the jumping bugs-that they're going to eat him. I've told him probably about fifty times that the bugs won't hurt him—but still he does not believe me. He's seen me squash them multiple times at Mom's urgent, demanding insistence of eradicating any creepy-crawly in the house within eyesight, and I wonder if that has affected him.

We went around this circle multiple times, until I came to the realization that we weren't going to fix the problem by rationalizing it away. Kids don't rationalize—Parents do, so I made up a story for Alex, that the bugs went to visit their mommy in Arizona - a place very, very far from here -and that it will be a long time before they come back. That seemed to work. I learned something valuable that day. If you can visualize your fears packing up and walking away, you can weaken and overcome them.

Later that week, I picked him up from daycare, arriving without him noticing me. He sat on the ground with his back to me playing with a toy. I stopped short, realizing it was the dreaded Jack-in-the-Box from my own childhood, come back to haunt me. Alex wound it up and as the lid sprung open, an action figure sailed across the room, propelled by the jack-in-the-box, turned catapult. I smiled. Just as I had helped Alex overcome his fears of the jumping bugs, he too had helped me overcome my discomfort by using the toy in a different way.

Sometimes, all you need is a child's innovation to launch your fears away.

~@~

Sunflower

He received it as a present, a packet of tiny dimly colored seeds,

Treasured from a special friend most dear.

Anxiously tugs at his father's sleeve,

"Plant it today, right here," he says, impatiently.

Tiny fingers clear the triangle mound,

Collecting leaves, worms and dirt.

Presses the shells one by one far down into the earth,

Depth of a smallish finger.

Lugs the watering can to the spigot, till filled quietly straining.

Caries it to the mound with na'er whimper nor complaining.

Bathes the capsules with life ingredients.

Urges the seeds to grow, now if by command.

Day by day he passes, pleading with his mound,

The life inside not a sign to be found,

Despite the daily pleading,

Passion wanes for his simple task,

Tendering no results.

Forlorn glances turn to excited dances

Single verdant shoot breaks through

Keeps vigil day by day until golden petals form and bloom

Mirrors the father gardener cultivating his own offshoots.

~@~

The Cell phone Photographer

Toddlers are gadget kings. They can figure out just about any technology far quicker than any parent. If you have a personal communication device, just hand it to a child and within seconds, it will be using features you never even knew existed. Text messages, pictures, ringtones, you name it—it magically appears at their fingertips.

I'm no Luddite when it comes to technology, but there are many features I just never had a use for previously—like cell phone cameras. To me they were an extravagance and a superfluous unnecessary gizmo. I mean, if you've got a camera, you use the camera—you don't need to take cell phone pictures and email them to yourself to prove you know how to use a camera.

One day, we found a digital camera lying on the ground while we were out walking—a small Sony, which we handed to Alex and became his very prized possession. He carried it everywhere and started snapping pictures. In true paparazzi form, he lines us up on the screen, cocks his head slightly to the side, and tells us he wants to take our picture—and then in rapid-fire sequence, snaps off several in a row. After each one he shouts out, "Do it again. Do it again!" while rotating the camera in his hands to get a better shot.

**Monkey Garden at the National Zoo,
Photo by Alex, age 3**

Truth be told, he frames his photos just like his great- grandfather did, who spent his working years as an industrial photographer, taking stills and montages of equipment and buildings to use in company materials. In his later years, when others were moving on to computer-aided design, he still enjoyed the simplicity of a camera and film. They were comfortable in his hands. I'm certain, that his spirit guides the shots of his great-grandson, who only knew him briefly.

Port Discovery Storyteller, Photo by Alex, age 3

~@~

Cover Sparkles

In the dry coldness of a winter night, a new game is born—the game of Cover Sparkles. As a boy, my brother and I would race to our shared room, scramble into our flannel pajamas turn out the lights, and dive into bed. On the count of ONE... TWO... THREE we would throw the woolen blankets over our heads and begin pedaling furiously, our sock-covered feet moving rhythmically against the roof of our bed-cave, static electricity arcs bouncing all around us. We raced until one of us gave up, exhausted, the light dissipating as we collapsed in a heap back on the bed and the covers settling back to earth. A few minutes later, we'd start again and continue this game for the next hour or so, until we heard someone – usually mom—yell at us to quit playing around and go to sleep.

Somewhere along the way, the magic light arcs died. My brother and I no longer raced cover sparkles anymore. The light we created on our own gave way to other pursuits: radios snuck under the covers for ball games, late-night homework projects and other distractions robbed us of our light, until one day we had forgotten about the spark.

The spark, though, was not dead; it was merely dormant, waiting for a strong bond to reunite it.

I found that bond in another cold dry night as I put my son to bed. Tucking him in, he kicked away the covers, his impish energies re-igniting the spark as his covers hissed and crackled with static arcs. I covered his head again, and watched him discover the dancing mini-lightning bolts ignite, fed by his boundless energy. I picked him up out of bed and lay him on the floor next to me, covering us with his blanket. Together we raced, our swift feet making mercury wings to the laughs and uncontrollable giggles of father and son.

Over and over again, we raced the cover sparkles, until we panted from exhaustion. Peeking out from under the covers I again heard 'Mom'—a different voice this time, but the same speech, tone, and inflection shouting out "All right you two. Bedtime!"

In that small instant, the cover sparkles had worked their magic. I traveled back in time. I was 7 again.

~@~

Over the last four years, I have found that I often go back in time (not literally—though it would be nice to use a time machine to erase many of those "Oh-No" seconds that we all have had throughout our lives.). I go back in time to my own childhood and better understand where I came from and the challenges my own parents had when raising the three of us. I said earlier that the knowledge of fathers is not directly passed—instead it is passed like a riddle for us to figure out—and only when we have children of our own do we fully understand what they were trying to teach us.

Who knows? Maybe we listened to that advice, holding it deep inside dormant for all these years awaiting the spark of inspiration to unlock its secrets. I think that since Alex was born, I have again become the student, eager to learn—about myself. I found that re-envisioning childhood through the eyes of the child has helped me to better understand my role as parent, husband, and father.

So what have I learned?

I've learned that as adults, we are too much in a hurry to get somewhere, that we miss the beauty that surrounds us—whether it is the last rays of sunlight, a simple flower on the ground, or scribbles on the paper forming the first letters of words. To an outsider, they may be inconsequential—to a toddler, they can be everything in the world. It's important to listen to what they have to say—even if it's the most unusual story you have ever heard. I don't mean listen with a half-hearted smirk and a knowing side glance—surmising that we adults know more than the child speaking. We have to get down to his level and contemplate it from a spot three foot high. Everything looks different from that angle. Why shouldn't the thoughts be different too?

I've learned that the best thing we can do for our children is to love them, to show them how to do things, and to help them learn new skills. They may not get it on their own—but they have to try. As parents, I constantly find myself resisting the urge to do something for Alex, because it's quicker so I can get on with my tasks at hand. One day I know, I will not be around—and who will then tie his shoes if I do not teach him? He has been taught at a young age to be self-sufficient. I may not always appreciate his desire to be self-sufficient in the moment when he is being stubborn and resolute, wanting to do things his own way, but I see it as a small bump in the road to eventual independence.

I've learned that, like the Peanuts characters in the classroom when they hear garbled sounds coming from the teacher, our voices are like buzzing flies—and when they don't do what we have asked of them multiple times—it's not that they don't understand the question, it's that they may not have even heard us to begin with. We, as adults in the adult world expect to only have to be told once to do something—unless it's from your wife saying take out the garbage—in which case, it may require more than once for it to register in our brains. It takes longer for them to recognize that we are actually talking to them. Because they hear things differently, I am less quick to judge. I have acquired patience.

I've learned that the moments that I thought I have it all together, are those most likely to hand me a lesson in humility—and also the most rewarding. It forces me to re-evaluate many of the beliefs that I have come to understand. Being proven wrong is, ironically one of the happiest moments of my life.

I've learned that the best five minutes of every day are after we read together and get ready for bed. Sometimes all we have is five minutes of silence—but it is our silence, and no one can take it away from us. I look forward to those five minutes every night.

In many ways, raising a child is like an adult riding a toddler bike—with knobby knees flung far out to the side as we wobble, unsure. We attempt to push the pedals, but our force spins the wheels in place rather than moving forward. As we try to regain control, even the training wheels holding us up do not support. We stumble—over and over again—teetering on the edge of falling off. In contrast, the toddler does not have the weight of the world on their shoulders. They have not developed the excessive power, they simply push and go. Now, as Alex is getting older, just as his training wheels are getting ready to come off his bike, so too are my parenting training wheels ready to be retired. I made it through the frustrations and sleepless nights. I survived the late night feedings, experienced the wonder of the tender moments between him and I, and in the process learned a few things about myself. Push hard upon the pedals. Let our momentum carry us on, together.

~@~

18. Five Minutes

Within the room of the fading orange glow, a child closes not his eyes,

Insists on a story or two of pirates, trains, or spies,

Crawls under the covers and leans over saucer- eyed,

Rests head upon his hands folded peacefully on the dimly lit pillow,

Impatiently waiting,

Urges Dad to utter the words that brings the day to close,

"What did you like best about today?"

Every day the answer astounds,

Dad Desperately In Need of Training Wheels

Some by its simplicity, others by complexity,

And others for adventure all around,

Talking of many things,

This bond of father and son,

Relates to me his dreams, even those which scare,

Enraptures me with his stories till he's said all he can care,

One by one the saucers narrow, gently drifting off to sleep,

In those five minutes, the secrets that we keep,

His, the secrets of sharing the best of his day with me,

Mine, listening to those stories he willingly shares.

~@~

Paul A. Stankus

About the Cover Illustrator

Gaithersburg, MD resident **Blanca Cervantes** is a butt-kicking graphic artist and aspiring children's book illustrator. When not drawing or attending classes, she can be found practicing her karate moves and playing video games. Originally drawing inspiration from Japanese anime, she is perfecting her own artistic style. Her favorite music styles are Power Metal and Chiptune.

About the Author

Rockville, MD resident **Paul A. Stankus** is a train scribe who can usually be found composing in the last car of DC Metro's Red Line. Over the last six years, he has written over 200 short stories, poems, and two books during his 45 minute each way daily commute to a quasi-non-profit in Washington DC.

Paul leads a weekly virtual poetry jam called DreadPoet's Storytime. In three years, it has grown from a handful of participants to over a hundred daily attendees who shout out a name, a place, and an action for the DreadPoet to compose a poem on the spot. He has written over 130 impromptu verses.

Paul is always on the look-out for what he terms, "the theatre of the absurd"—those real-life moments that are often stranger than fiction.

Made in the USA
Charleston, SC
14 January 2013